1

The Anthology Question
What is the exam?

For some, poetry can be the most intimidating part of the Literature GCSE. But it doesn't have to be! The Poetry Anthology is examined on AQA English Literature Paper 2, Section B.

I think that the poetry section is the easiest to prepare for:

- There's less content than other sections.
- One of the anthology poems is printed on the paper.
- You know all the potential questions.
- The timing is quite generous, once you have a good essay structure.

MYTHS ABOUT POETRY EXAMS

There are so many things people say about poetry that just aren't true.

Myth: I have to memorise all fifteen
Truth: No, you don't

Think about that for a moment. You don't have to learn all the key Shakespeare speeches, or four chapters of your novel by heart. I don't know where this came from, but it's not true.

You <u>do</u> need to:

1. Know the poems well
2. Know their themes and ideas
3. Know some quotations

It's better to be selective and thoughtful when revising quotations than recite huge chunks.

It's true that the better you understand the poem the better you'll do. But learning it by heart won't help. In fact, if you just wrote out the poem, you'd pretty much get 0 marks.

Myth: Poetry is hard
Truth: It can be. But poetry analysis can be learned

It's tricky at first when it's unfamiliar or you don't have a way in. You're likely to have read novels, and perhaps seen or read plays before. You'll have 'done' poetry at school but probably don't sit down and read poetry for pleasure – so you're just less experienced with it.

Poetry is dense. Space is limited, so every word fights for its place by adding meaning. And unlike novels, which are mostly about characters doing things, poetry is more often about ideas or moments of feeling.

Myth: There's so much technique to learn
Truth: Not more than any other text

It's easy to be intimidated by glossaries and long lists of words. It is true, as we look at later, that academic, ambitious language can go a long way.

But understanding poems and explaining word choices is more important than labelling techniques.

Myth: Learning it is so difficult
Truth: You learn new things every day, all the time

Think of all the songs you can sing by heart, the film and TV quotations you can recite without thinking. You can memorise and learn! Part of the trick is to show your brain that memorising *this* is important – which is covered in the Revision section.

WHAT DO YOU REALLY HAVE TO DO?

For the anthology question, it is simple:

Write an essay comparing the way that two of the poems from the anthology explore a given theme.

The list of poems will be printed on the paper.

The named poem you must use will be printed.

You then choose a poem to compare it with.

It's a good idea to spend time planning the anthology essay:

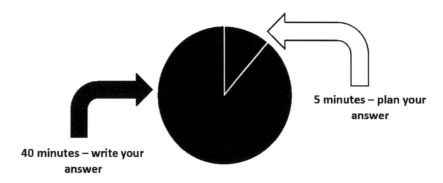

40 minutes – write your answer

5 minutes – plan your answer

The question is worth 30 marks, or 20% of the GCSE.

We'll cover essay structure in a later section, but a good guideline is to write between 2-3 sides for a high-grade answer[1]. This is a reasonable amount in 45 minutes. It won't be everything you know about the poems either; exams are a snapshot of what you know, so it's important to be organised.

In summer 2018, the grade boundary equivalents were:[2]

Grade			Grade		
	9	25 marks		6	17 marks
	8	23		5	14
	7	20		4	11

Over the whole GCSE boundaries were about 15 marks apart – but this isn't a big difference when split between the questions. I find this very encouraging: it's easy to pick up a few extra marks and skip up the mark-scheme!

In the next section, you'll learn what the mark-scheme really means and what examiners are looking for in a great essay.

The key to getting grade 7+ is to make sure that your argument is thoughtful and developed, and that you're always examining rather than explaining.

The first half of this book will help you look at the more complex ideas in the poetry, and to express yourself in an analytical way.

Then, in the second half, there are plenty of model answers to read, to see what examiners are looking for, and questions to practise for yourself.

QUICK QUIZ:
4. When is the anthology examined?
5. How many minutes is the poetry anthology question?
6. What is printed on the paper?
7. How much should you aim to write?
8. How should you divide your time?
9. What are the key words in the mark-scheme?

---

[1] Cambridge University did some research into high-grade English essays at GCSE, and found that the candidates who got the equivalent of 7+ wrote 650-700 words on average.
http://www.cambridgeassessment.org.uk/Images/426173-how-much-do-i-need-to-write-to-get-top-marks-.pdf
[2] Grade boundaries are calculated across the whole exam, but it can be useful to think about how many marks you need in each question. Remember that grade boundaries change a little every year as well.

Understanding the mark-scheme

AO1: Read, understand and respond to texts. (12 marks)
Students should be able to:

- maintain a critical style and develop an informed personal response
- use textual references, including quotations, to support and illustrate interpretations.

AO2: Analyse the language, form and structure used by a writer to create meanings and effects, using relevant subject terminology where appropriate. (12 marks)

AO3: Show understanding of the relationships between texts and the contexts in which they were written. (6 marks)

Level 6		Convincing, critical analysis and exploration 26–30 marks	**AO1** • Critical, exploratory comparison • Judicious use of precise references to support interpretation(s) **AO2** • Analysis of writer's methods with subject terminology used judiciously • Exploration of effects of writer's methods on reader **AO3** • Exploration of ideas/perspectives/contextual factors shown by specific, detailed links between context/text/task
Level 5	Grade 9 – 25 marks Grade 8 – 23 marks	Thoughtful, developed consideration 21–25 marks	**AO1** • Thoughtful, developed comparison • Apt references integrated into interpretation(s) **AO2** • Examination of writer's methods with subject terminology used effectively to support consideration of methods • Examination of effects of writer's methods on reader **AO3** • Thoughtful consideration of ideas/perspectives/contextual factors shown by examination of detailed links between context/text/task

Level 4	Grade 7 – 20 marks	Clear understanding 16-20 marks	**AO1** • Clear comparison • Effective use of references to support explanation **AO2** • Clear explanation of writer's methods with appropriate use of relevant subject terminology • Understanding of effects of writer's methods on reader **AO3** • Clear understanding of ideas/perspectives/ contextual factors shown by specific links between context/text/task
	Grade 6 – 17 marks		
Level 3	Grade 5 – 14 marks	Explained, Structured comments 11-15 marks	**AO1** • Some explained comparison • References used to support a range of relevant comments. **AO2** • Explained/relevant comment on writer's methods with some relevant use of subject terminology • Identification of effects of writer's methods on reader **AO3** • Some understanding of ideas/perspectives/ contextual factors shown by specific links between context/text/task
	Grade 4 – 11 marks		

WHAT ARE THE ASSESSMENT OBJECTIVES?

AO1: This is about your ideas, argument, and answering the question.

- Do you know the poems well?
- Do you see the themes and ideas of a poem?
- Can you explore their subjects, meanings and ideas in detail?
- Can you compare the poems' representation of ideas?
- Can you be selective in choosing what you write about?
- Is your writing clear, precise, and purposeful?
- Is your essay structure helping your ideas to come across well?

AO2: This focuses on your analysis of the writer's techniques: how they are creating their sense of meaning.

- Can you identify some of the most interesting or important sections of the poem to explore?
- Can you explore how a writer works?
- Do you 'get' that a writer works hard to craft their work, shaping it deliberately and making precise choices that convey what they want to say?
- Can you explore a variety of language techniques?
- Can you look at the structure of the poem and understand the writer's choices?
- Can you explain, where relevant, the way that the form of the poem affects the meaning?
- Do you know some literary vocabulary that can help to precisely explain your interpretation?
- Can you use this fluently rather than just labelling sentences?

AO3: Here, you need to show knowledge of themes and ideas. Some context is useful (social, literary and historical).

- Can you explore the way writers look at similar themes or ideas, exploring the different ways they approach them?
- Can you recognise, where important, differences such as time period, attitude towards relationships, expectations (e.g. of gender roles or relationships), or the way that different forms of poems might be chosen to have different impacts?

SO, WHAT DO I DO NEXT?

Level 3: 11-15 marks

You clearly explain what you think and why you think it.

To get Grade 5 (at the top of level 3), there's more sense that you know the writer is working purposefully on effect – that they have deliberately chosen their words and organisation. You must explain what some of these choices are.

In level 3, students identify effects, often in some more basic ways with language like "positive" or "sad" rather than something more precise like "joyful" or "quietly optimistic," "reflective" or "nostalgic".

Writing structures are more formulaic or repetitive, for example always using Point – Evidence – Explain or Point – Evidence – Analysis in a straightforward way.

You're writing about content rather than construction. You might write about what characters in the poem are doing, or the story of the poem. This can feel like you're focused (e.g. the Farmer's unhappiness changes through the poem) but because you don't explain why the writer's doing that, it's not developed. Working through the poem from start to end is also a level 3 characteristic.

WAYS TO IMPROVE:

- Use more precise vocabulary e.g. "pessimistic" instead of "negative"
- Regularly use the writer's name to show you're focused on technique *e.g. "Browning shows that Porphyria is…"*
- Use technical language to focus on the writer's construction.
- Use examples from different parts of the poem *e.g. Shelley uses natural imagery – water in stanza 1 and flowers in stanza 2*. This shows you're looking at the whole poem rather than working in chronological order.

Level 4: 16-20 marks

You know what the poem is "about" related to themes or ideas, rather than plot, character or theme. Most of your points will be about this idea; instead of simply choosing a few quotations they'll all be connected through a theme.

Your writing is more developed at a paragraph level. You can put a phrase under a microscope and explain the connotations or underlying meaning.

You can zoom back out of a quotation, linking it somewhere else or beginning to explain why it matters.

You're more focused on the writer's technique and construction; there'll be more analysis of the technical aspects of writing rather than writing about character or story.

WAYS TO IMPROVE:

- Start with a theme *e.g. Hardy shows the bitterness of ending a relationship* and focus your answer on how that is being done. This means being selective, so it's important to remember that your exam is just a snapshot, not all your knowledge.
- Use micro-quotations (just a word or two, rather than full lines). Link several quotations together from different points of the poem.
- Use topic sentences for your paragraphs that use the "**technique** – <u>purpose</u>" structure e.g. "Mew uses **imagery of the seasons** to structure her poem, exploring the changes over the course of the relationships."
- Each paragraph should have several micro-quotations, explored and linked together.
- A conclusion will bring the two poems together, comparing the writer's message or purpose related to the question.

Level 5: 21-25 marks

At the top of this level, you will start with an idea or theme and explore the writer's response to it.

Your paragraphs will be longer and more developed. The topic sentences will be based on theme or idea. Topic sentences might use the "technique – purpose" structure (see box above).

You'll be looking at patterns of language across the poem, not working from beginning to end. Think of it as stepping back and seeing the whole poem. You'll link quotations together that contribute to an idea.

You'll be writing about technique - the impact of language deliberately chosen. Some of this will be tentative, showing that you know there are multiple interpretations.

Your quote choices will be precise, often shorter – even a word or two - and peppered through your writing rather than using a strict PEA structure.

WAYS TO IMPROVE:

- Create an argument that compares the poems e.g. one is bitter, one is optimistic, or that links to the contexts of the poets – a perspective from a parent is different to that of a child.
- Make paragraphs ideas focused e.g. Sheers explores the fragility of relationships.
- Then, choose several techniques with different evidence to support your ideas.
- Offer alternatives – ask questions or suggest different readings (e.g. is the farmer angry or despairing, and how are these possibilities conveyed)
- Use tentative language like could, might, maybe, perhaps

Level 6: 26-30 marks

The defining characteristic is that an answer here will have a strong argument – you'll know what you want to say about a poem from a conceptual viewpoint (understanding its ideas) and your whole essay is about discussing this argument.

Analysis will be precise, fine grained, and exploratory. Your choice of quotations will be very specific, and there's a feeling that it's exactly the right way to illustrate your argument.

Your evidence will come from across the text, with examples drawn from different places and clustered together.

Sometimes you'll be comparing based on technique, sometimes on idea.

Your writing will be clear, precise, and purposeful.

QUICK QUIZ:
1. What are the different assessment objectives looking at?
2. What is the usual structure of a level 3 response?
3. What is the defining characteristic of a level 6 response?
4. What distinguishes a level 4 or 5 answer from level 3?
5. What should you start with for a level 5 response?
6. How should you look at language for a level 5 response?

What to look for in poetry

Although most of this book is about the anthology, the way that you study the fifteen anthology poems is superb practice for the unseen section. When you're approaching any poem for the first time, the tips below should help.

Read it slowly.

Including the title.

What's it about? How does it feel? What stands out to you? Don't feel you have to annotate anything yet.

Start with the basics. Make sure you know who's talking. Who are they talking to, and what about? Is it a conversation with a specific person or a moment in time that's being described? Does the title give you any clues? What feelings are there in the poem?

Find the change.

Poems often involve a moment of change – when something happens, or the narrator comes to understand something.

Look at the difference between the beginning and end lines. What happens? Does the speaker realise something? Is there a change in tone or feeling? Or is there a lack of change?

Slow down.

Go back to the beginning, with the starting understanding that you have, and try to imagine it being read aloud.

Underline phrases, words, or images that seem important or interesting – even if you don't know why.

Zoom into the detail.

For each of your underlined quotations, add a couple of quick notes:

What do they mean?

What feeling are they expressing?

What techniques are there? (not every quotation will have a technique associated with it and that's ok. Being able to explore the impact of the phrasing is more important.)

Do they connect with another quotation somewhere else?

Rhyme / rhythm

Is there a rhyme scheme? If so, which words are being put together? In Sections 3 and 4 we'll have a look at how to analyse this in more detail.

Try to 'hear' the poem in your head. Think about where the rhythm is obvious. For example: is there a place where words seem to be in the opposite order to what you might expect, to fit a pattern? Are there words that become emphasised through a rhythm? Which words on each line seem to be emphasised more?

This isn't about identifying pentameter or trimeter – although you can if you know it and what you say is purposeful – but you need to see how the poem feels when read aloud, and which words the writer is drawing attention to.

Patterns

You'll probably have noticed this by now, but is there a pattern of language?

Are there words associated with the same idea? Is there an image that is used more than once, especially if it changes through the poem? Is there a theme like nature, religion, or death that you can identify?

EXAM TIP:
It's useful to circle and connect these on your paper so you can easily find them when writing

---

SIX STEPS OF POETRY ANNOTATION:

1. Read
2. Find the change
3. Slow down
4. Zoom in
5. Rhyme/rhythm
6. Pattern

OTHER WAYS TO GET INTO A POEM:

Change it

Read the poem ignoring the line breaks – read by sentence, like you would a novel paragraph. This can make it easier to see the ideas behind it.

Crunch it

For every line, decide THE most important word. This can be a great way to select language to analyse too: simply explain why it's important.

Split it

Decide where you split the poem into rough thirds – beginning, middle, end. Use this to look for the change and explore the structure of the poem.

QUICK QUIZ:
1. What are the 6 steps to analysing a poem?
2. What are three other ways to get into a poem?

Analysing metaphor

Metaphor is one of the poet's most important tools – and essential for a top-grade student to understand.

At its most simple, metaphor is just this: using one idea to stand in for another.

We use it every day. Look at some of these examples:

In poetry, you might find either a single metaphor in a single sentence or an extended metaphor that continues across one or more stanzas.

Here are some metaphors that are commonly used by poets. There's no way to write all of them here, but these will help you get familiar with some of the ideas used in literary works and provide a starting point. The second column gives you some suggestions for what it might represent – but remember that this is just a starting point. Some poets might use them to subvert your usual expectations.

Understanding is vision

Ideas are **clear**, **bright**, **dim**, **fuzzy**, **colourful**. They are **illuminated**. If you see what I mean.

Life is a journey

We've all heard it. Language of **the destination being less important than the journey**, the **emotional rollercoaster**, the path we want to find ourselves on, seeing the **signs** in our lives to get us there.

Emotions are diseases or movement

We find humour **infectious**, are **overpowered** by our feelings. We're **lovesick**, **knocked out** when impressed or **plunged** into despair.

Metaphor	What might it mean?	Anthology example
Nature	Growth, life, the promise of regeneration	Love's Philosophy: the pairing of the natural elements and their gradual increase in size symbolises the 'natural' love that could grow between them.
Trees	Strength, longevity – a sense that the tree will outlive the speaker.	Sonnet 29: the broad trunk of the speaker's lover promises strength and virility.
Flowers	Beauty – but often fleeting or short-lived. Specific flowers might also have individual connotations, for example: roses/love; lily/death.	The Farmer's Bride: holly berries for Christmas, with the red as a symbol of hope in the depths of winter but they also ironically emphasise his despair over their lack of children, or their lack of 'fruitfulness'.
Birds	Freedom (association with flight). Different birds might have different meanings, e.g. owls – wise, but also quite cruel and secretive; wren – small, plain, vulnerable.	Letters from Yorkshire: Lapwings signify the return of spring, and therefore the warmth of the relationship being maintained.
The moon / the sun	Compare the strength of the light, e.g. the moon is weaker. The moon is also a more feminine symbol, due to its association with the monthly cycle. The moon might represent changeability – it waxes and wanes. The sun, however, is stronger and a reminder of the continuity of life – but also perhaps overpowering.	Neutral Tones: the sun is "curst" and weaker than it should be, unable to provide the warmth and solace it usually would.
Cold	Isolation; death or loneliness; depression.	When We Two Parted: the semantic field of cold echoes the loneliness since the relationship ended.
Light / dark	Secrets and uncovering them; good and evil; happiness and misery – the sense of contrast is often the most important thing. There might be, for example, a contrast between light and dark, or between important thing. There might be, for example, a contrast between light and dark, or between types of light, like a candle and a fire.	Singh Song!: the silver moonlight at the end is a romanticised image emphasising the speaker's attitude towards their relationship.
Heat	Passion; love; togetherness; fulfilment. If it's too hot, though, look for discomfort or signs of hell elsewhere.	Walking Away: the firing of the clay refers to being hardened or finished in the kiln, being seared in the heat changes them and makes them stronger.

Metaphor	What might it mean?	Anthology example
Death	Endings – not necessarily physical death, but the endings of relationships or moments in life. Imagery of death can be related to the person's body, their feelings, or the rituals of death like ringing the death knell, funeral rites etc.	Porphyria's Lover: although Porphyria does literally die, the metaphor here could be of control, the power of the lover and by extension the patriarchal society that polices female sexuality.
Spring	Rebirth and growth, new life and fertility.	Letters from Yorkshire: the letters explain the coming of spring and the renewal of communication in the relationship
Summer	Heat; love; passion; bliss.	Eden Rock: the blissful peaceful nature of the scene is suggestive of heaven.
Autumn	Harvest; fertility; fulfilment of promise.	The Farmer's Bride: the couple marry in the autumn, when there is promise of the 'harvest' and fertility in the relationship as well as nature, but this hope quickly disappears.
Winter	Dying as nature dies; cold; isolation and loneliness.	Winter Swans: the potentially impending death of the relationship.
Journey	Decisions being taken; direction being sought; look at what it being moved towards and away from.	Mother, Any Distance: the space exploration represents the increasing distance as well as the potential danger – and excitement – of the speaker's changing relationship with his mother.
Water	Rebirth and cleansing, drawing on baptism rites; crossing over into death (using rivers from Greek myth which were the boundary between the world and the underworld)	Eden Rock: the speaker must 'cross over' the river to the world of the dead where his parents reside.
Time	Passing by; whether it's used well or is slipping too fast; drawing attention to the single moment or a long period.	The Farmer's Bride: the seasons represent the deterioration of the relationship.
Colours	Think of the obvious, such as red of for passion and anger, but red might also symbolise Christmas or excitement and glamour.	Before You Were Mine: the mother's red high heels represent her sexualised glamour and an outgoing, flirtatious personality.
Snakes / serpents	Evil, drawing on Biblical allusions to Satan's temptation in the Garden of Eden.	Not in the Anthology, but a common metaphor elsewhere.

QUICK QUIZ:
1. Work through the Anthology poems and identify a metaphor being used, with a quick comment about what it represents. Some might be from the table above.

What is "context?"

Context means understanding where the text fits into its historical[3], thematic, and literary place.[4]

Historical

How does the poem fit into a socio-historical place and time – and how do different audiences in different societies and times view its ideas?

Does the poem reflect attitudes about relationships that are typical of its era, or is it beginning to challenge these stereotypes?

Does the poet's personal history have an impact on the poem?

Thematic

How do writers from different backgrounds and experiences write about the same themes?

With the love and relationships anthology, themes could include:

- Power balance in the relationship
- Strength of the relationship
- How well the lovers communicate
- Distance, emotional and physical
- Changing relationships
- Relationships that have ended, and how each person feels about this
- What "romance" is and how it's conveyed
- How people show that they love one another
- Ideas about fate or destiny
- Whether relationships live up to the ideals of those involved

Literary

How does the writer fit into the traditions of literature?

Does the poem fit into a particular genre?

Does the writer often use similar themes, imagery or ideas?

If the poet is in a 'school' of poetry like Romantic, do they use those traditional styles in this poem?

Do writers use traditional images (e.g. metaphors of nature, light) in different or similar ways to one another?

What has influenced the writers' style?

> **EXAM TIP:**
> Context always has to be connected to the text. Don't be tempted to add a final sentence on the end of a paragraph, or suddenly throw in a random fact.

---

[3] You'll see references to social, historical and literary. I tend to think of "social" and "historical" as being the same thing.

[4] In a longer text like the Shakespeare or 19th century novel, it can also mean where in the text something happens and why it's important at that moment.

For example:

Elizabeth Barrett Browning was an invalid and often bed-bound so wrote this to her lover Robert.

This is perfectly true historical context. But it doesn't explain anything about the poem's meaning or themes. However…

Elizabeth Barrett Browning was an invalid and often bed-bound; writing to her lover Robert, we can see some anxiety about her feeling needy or uncertain, describing herself as a "wild vine" which is "straggling green" – the "straggling" sound unhealthy, even weak. This might also have caused her to fear that she was smothering Robert, as "there's naught to see" but the "wild vine" as her thoughts tangle around him in his absence.

This takes the information and looks for whether it might have some significance, in this case that because Barrett Browning was unwell she might have felt lonely or missed her lover, or felt her thoughts tended towards jealousy as a result of their separation.

> **REVISION TASK:**
> For each poem make a note of 2-3 contextual points.

QUICK QUIZ:
1. What are the three types of context?
2. How should context NOT be used?

Academic Writing
Improving your essay writing

There are lots of different factors involved in writing well, and it does take dedicated practice. Writing practice is essential, but don't just sit down and knock out a series of 45-minute essays without thinking.

Exam timing is important but needs separate practice.

Writing practice means working more slowly, redrafting, thinking about how to improve your individual sentences and paragraphs.

Great writing is also a way of thinking. You're not writing about the whole poem – you're writing about an aspect of the poem, choosing the bits that fit what you want to say about it.

You might find the list below a bit intimidating at first. That's ok – writing is a skill that takes time to develop.

Take one or two of the techniques below and practise them. When you get confident with them, add another.

WHAT MAKES GREAT ACADEMIC WRITING?

- **Velcro paragraphs** that fit together, in the right order, leading the reader through the argument
- **A critical argument** that incorporates a 'big picture' of literature
- Focused and purposeful writing that doesn't veer off-topic
- **A confident writing voice**, using an academic register
- **A compelling conclusion** that draws everything together and makes your answer to the question clear.
- **Embedded quotations** that are exactly right for the point being made
- Academic interpretive vocabulary that doesn't waffle
- **Literary vocabulary** that is precise and used effectively
- **Mechanical competence** – the spelling, punctuation and grammar is always accurate

The following pages will give you more guidance on some of these different aspects.

QUICK QUIZ:
1. What is important about exam timing vs. writing practice?
2. What two types of vocabulary are important?

Introductions: writing an argument

A strong argument is a critical factor in writing well.

With one, your writing is purposeful, paragraphs flow one to the next and you sound focused.

Without it, you either have a series of disconnected points or work chronologically through the poem spotting techniques and ideas without really exploring the cohesive whole.

In the poetry comparison, you need to establish what the poems have in common and why they are different.

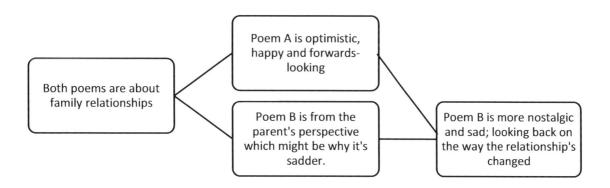

Read through some of these introductions, taken from the model essays at the end of this book.

All of them have several things in common:

1. The poems are both named
2. The poems are linked with broad themes related to the question which will then be narrowed, e.g. "distance" divides into "physical" and "emotional".
3. They focus on the writer's purpose or message, not the character. When the characters are mentioned, for example Porphyria's Lover, it's as a construct by the writer.
4. They use a wide range of interpretive adjectives e.g. turbulent, obsessive, heart-breaking, finite.
5. They all mention the contexts' impact on the difference between the poems.

Context at start, confident statement

Despite their different genders and writing nearly 80 years apart, Browning and Mew both explore the problematic nature of the patriarchal, unequal society in which they lived. Browning's Lover is obsessive to the point of destruction, driven mad in part by a need to possess a woman who exercises unusual authority for the time and makes him feel powerless. Mew's farmer has disturbing hints, at the end, of a similar obsession, yet Mew's sympathetic portrayal suggests that his desperation is borne of a society which demands women marry – and lose much of their freedom in the process – yet also insists men and women can't genuinely get to know one another before marriage.

Critical academic voice, linking patriarchal society to the influence it has on the poets.

Ambitious vocabulary to interpret the character. Connects with the patriarchal system established as a factor - context.

Comparison of characters using same vocabulary ("obsession")

Uses context as a reason for the story of the poem

Personification of 'society' creates detached tone. Subordinate clause creates a sophisticated academic register

---

Both poems named with a broad similarity – "distance" is the question

'The Farmer's Bride' and 'Letters from Yorkshire' explore different kinds of distance. The emotional distance between the farmer and his bride in Charlotte Mew's poem represents the misery of a marriage without love or communication. In 'Letters from Yorkshire', communication is crucial in maintaining a relationship that instead suffers from a physical distance.

Each poem has a sentence of explanation – even the introduction is balanced.

Comparison is clear – physical vs. emotional distance.

Sophisticated vocabulary of interpretation

The poets are named quickly,

For Byron and Hardy, love is misery. With their own turbulent romantic lives and their literary focus on the downtrodden and miserable, it is no surprise that these romance poems also explore the unending, heart-breaking, soul-destroying side of love.

Strong confident statement

Triadic structure of adjectives suggests confidence of interpretation. Very strong language shows confidence.

Brief context; it's clear this will be developed later. Shows a wider understanding of the poets' lives and work

Starting with the named poem, identifying the theme (children growing up like their parents).

In 'Follower', Heaney explores the way that children follow in their parents' metaphorical – and literal – footsteps. Through its extended metaphors, the speaker considers how parents forge a path, shaping the world around them, and the ways that children must then interpret their own movement through the world either re-forging their parents' paths or creating a new one. In 'Before You Were Mine', Carol Ann Duffy also reflects on how children look at their parents. In her poem, Duffy memorialises her mother but acknowledges her understanding is finite: her imagination must fill in the gaps of her mother's life.

Brief technical detail which will be picked up later.

The sentence uses its own metaphor to explain children following their parents' patterns.

Comparison links back to the theme

Verb choice "memorialises" is more sophisticated than "remembers"; suggests the poem is a way of creating a memory too.

REVISION TASK:

Get some of your old essays, re-read them and redraft the introduction to create a stronger argument.

DECIDING WHAT YOUR ARGUMENT SHOULD BE

To be able to write an introduction like this you need to explore the themes of the poetry in more detail.

Try to think of it like this; if you had to summarise the poem's idea in one sentence, what would it be?

Don't get distracted into narrative story-telling or describing the characters. Instead, think about what the characters represent about society, relationships, attitudes and so on.

For example, the Farmer's Bride is not just a poem about a failing marriage. Writing about it this way is more likely to be a Level 3 answer.

Instead, it could be about:

- People's inability to communicate in intimate relationships
- The possible tragic outcome of marriages where the couple don't really know one another
- A society where marriages are arranged, or made because they are 'suitable', rather than made for love.
- The way different types of people are incompatible.
- Social expectations of relationships
- Male power and control in marriage
- Rural communities' expectations of marriage

In all of these examples, the farmer and the bride are characters who could represent many people in their society. They are generic characters, rather than individuals – while we are supposed to empathise with them from a story-telling perspective, we are also supposed to empathise with others in their position.

REVISION TASK:

Make a list of thematic sentences for each of the poems in the anthology. This can be the starting point for your pairings.

QUICK QUIZ:
1. Why is an argument good?
2. What are the 5 ingredients of a good introduction?
3. How could you decide on the theme of the poem?

Writing in an academic way

WHAT IS AN ACADEMIC REGISTER?

Register is about the tone and formality of your writing. It's the difference between an essay and a letter, a story and an email. Each subject has its own register, too – you'll need a different tone and different key words in Biology, Geography, and English.

English examiners like a bit of flair and creativity in their writing, even the essays! Reading an essay that's interestingly written makes it more enjoyable, but also suggests that the student enjoyed writing it – which shows that they feel confident in what they're writing. You don't want to slip into informality, but you do want to be interesting when you write.

A good academic register:

- Uses the writers' full names or surnames, never just their first name
- Uses writing techniques to create a personal voice, e.g. using metaphor, triadic structures of adjectives
- Uses adjectives to develop interpretation
- Avoid the word "quote"
- Uses more interesting connectives (yet, despite, although, therefore)
- Has a range of words for "shows" or "write"
- Uses subordinate clauses to add commentary or detail

Look at this example from one of the model essays:

Sheers and Hardy both use imagery of water as the central theme to explore the anguish of their relationships. At the opening of Neutral Tones, the speaker reflects: "we stood by a pond that winter day." The stagnant water of the pond, unmoved by currents or tides, is reflected in the cyclical nature of the poem which returns to the image at the end, now with the "pond edged with greyish leaves." Nothing has changed in the relationship; they remain separated, but in pain. Sheers' couple, too, begin beside water albeit initially more disturbed and potentially threatening, as the "waterlogged earth gulped for breath" beside the lake. Personifying the struggling ground represents the conflicts within the relationship, the couple gasping for air despite the suffocation of the "storms" that have raged for two days. Yet Sheers allows some optimism to creep in; there's a "break in which we walked" offering a chance of reconciliation – is it possible that the storms, or arguments, will be amicably resolved? Or is the undertone instead suggesting a more ominous and permanent "break"? Lakes, however, unlike ponds, have currents and move, perhaps indicating that the couple may be able to move on from their trauma.

- The student uses rhetorical questions to suggest tentative alternative interpretations.
- Interpretive language includes anguish, cyclical, disturbed, threatening, struggling, suffocation, optimism, raged, amicably.
- Connectives used include yet, however.
- The poets reflect, allow and suggest rather than show.
- There are four embedded quotations, some of which have sections repeated as the student zooms into analysis.

HOW DO I IMPROVE MY WRITING?

Practising lexical density can be very helpful. This is about making every word count and reducing any waffle. By reducing the quantity that you write, you are forced to improve the quality of your writing at a sentence level.

Look at this worked example:

In Climbing My Grandfather, Andrew Waterhouse uses an extended metaphor of climbing to represent the way that he wants to understand his grandfather more and develop their relationship. He does this because he was an environmentalist and naturalist and enjoyed the outdoors. He uses the quotation "I decide to do it free, without a net." This starts the metaphor and shows that he is taking a chance without knowing how it will all turn out.

(75 words)

This is fine – the information is all accurate, and there's some useful comments about the context of the poet, the techniques being used, and the writer's intention.

Writing-wise, however, it's a little plodding. The sentences don't quite flow together, and it could have more embedded interpretation.

A re-write would look like this:

As a keen environmentalist, Waterhouse uses the extended metaphor of climbing to represent his desire to understand his grandfather, beginning with the opening line "I decide to do it free, without a net." Aware of the risks of a close relationship, Waterhouse knows that – like climbing – there is no safety net when getting to know someone.

(56 words)

This is about 20 words shorter, for a start, and conveys more or less the same information but sounds much more confident. So, what changed?

- Sentence starters – instead of "he or "this", using "as" and "aware" make sentences more interesting.
- Subordinate clauses at the start of the sentences adding interest
- Subordinate clause "like climbing" emphasises the connection between Waterhouse's metaphor and his personal interests.
- Precision of vocabulary – "desire" replaces "the way that he wants to", and "as a keen environmentalist" replaced the long contextual sentence in the middle, which is sort of stuck into the first paragraph rather than applied. Using "as" shows a clear connection to the poet's ideas.

HOW TO PRACTICE THIS:

Reduce the word-count to start with

Word-count isn't everything, by any means, but by forcing yourself to cut 20% of your words, you force yourself to focus on conveying the same information in a more concise way

Use the techniques above

The list at the beginning of the section is a good place to start. Try working your way through different techniques and see how they change your writing style.

Change your sentence starters

Removing basic pronouns (he, she, they, this). Start with a verb or adjective instead and see what happens.

Don't do this for a whole essay! At least not at first. Practice should be small-scale, working on a paragraph at a time. Challenge yourself to make an individual paragraph as good as you can.

When you feel confident, think about moving onto an essay - but even then, I usually work a paragraph at a time.

You won't do this in an exam - you don't have time to redraft. The point here is to practise your writing style **throughout** your studying. That way, when you get to the exam you will already have a confident academic style of writing.

REVISION TASK:

Use some of your recent writing to practice cutting your word count by 20%.

QUICK QUIZ:
1. What does "register" mean?
2. Suggest three ways to improve academic register.
3. What is "lexical density"?
4. What 2 things could help practise this?
5. How much should I do?

How to embed quotations

Level 6 of the mark-scheme asks you to demonstrate "judicious use of precise reference to support interpretations." For Level 5 and above, they need to be "integrated into interpretations".

As we said earlier, this means:

1. Choosing exactly the right word/phrase to prove your point
2. Embedding the quotation fluently

Embedding quotations is a crucial part of writing in an academic way for GCSE and A-Level.

Essentially, a quotation is embedded if the sentence reads fluently.

Have a look at some of these examples:

Singh Song!

Nagra describes the way the bride behaves. We know this because he quotes "effing at my mum."

The writer doesn't 'quote'. Quoting is repetition of something that someone else has said. Readers quote writers. Writers write.

This also doesn't need to be separated into two sentences

Instead, it should be:

Nagra describes the bride as "effing at my mum."

This is more fluent: we don't have a break between the analytical comment and the quotation.

Or:

Nagra explores the clash of cultural expectations as the bride is "effing at my mum."

This embeds analysis at the beginning – the clash of cultural expectations – and then uses the quotation as an example to illustrate the point.

You can either say that the writer describes, or – as in this case – you can link the action to the character

When We Two Parted

Byron uses a semantic field of death to link to the gothic. "Sunk chill" and "sever" are examples of the semantic field.

This has the technical vocabulary, explanation of impact (the link to the gothic) and examples – so it's a good start.

However, it could be:

Byron's semantic field – "sunk chill", "sever" – creates an impression of gothic death.

- Using hyphens is a good way to include references to several quotations at once.
- Keep the quotations very short.
- Keep quotations connected – these are evidence of the semantic field.
- Select language from different places in the poem, to show that you are looking at patterns.

Follower:

This awkwardness is transferred from son to father at the end. This is seen in the quotation "today/it is my father who keeps stumbling/...and will not go away."

- The use of "quotation" is a little clunky.
- It's also quite a length quotation to use and might be better cut down.
- However, if it is all relevant, then it can be added onto the end of an analytical sentence.

Instead:

This awkwardness, however, is transferred to the father by the end of the poem as their roles have reversed: "today/it is my father who keeps stumbling/...and will not go away."

- Using a colon at the end of the analysis links the quotation.
- Generally avoid quotations longer than this. They're harder to learn, but you're also less likely to be really using all of them.
- After a longer quotation like this one, try to zoom into it and explore a key word, for example "stumbling" here.

WAYS TO EMBED QUOTATIONS:

1. Fluently into the sentence, a word or two at a time
2. As a short list between hyphens
3. At the end of a sentence, after a colon

QUICK QUIZ:
1. What is an embedded quotation?
2. What are three ways to embed quotations?

REVISION TASK:

Using an old essay, look for an quotes that aren't embedded and re-write the sentences.

Comma splicing

Comma splicing is a very common grammatical error when two independent clauses are joined together with a comma.

An independent clause makes sense on its own.

Example: Charlotte Mew explores the farmer's misery; the bride makes him miserable.

These are the two clauses:

1. Charlotte Mew explores the farmer's misery.

2. The bride makes him miserable.

Each one makes sense on their own and so they don't need connecting with a comma. There are several alternatives:

1. Use a full stop.

Charlotte Mew explores the farmer's misery. The bride makes him miserable.

This is the simplest option, but often means you end up with a lot of very short sentences. This can make your writing seem 'choppy' and like you're not really connecting your ideas together.

2. Use a semi-colon

Charlotte Mew explores the farmer's misery; the bride makes him miserable.

Semi-colons join two independent clauses which creates a link between them – the two ideas in the clauses have to be connected like the example above.

Charlotte Mew explores the farmer's misery; the bride is like a hare.

In the above example, the semi-colon is grammatically accurate, but the two clauses don't really connect together, so a full stop would be more appropriate.

3. Use a word to connect the ideas

Charlotte Mew explores the farmer's misery, suggesting the bride makes him miserable.

4. Rephrase the sentences

Charlotte Mew explores the farmer's misery, caused by the bride.

COMMA SPLICING QUOTATIONS

One of the most common places to see comma splicing is after a quotation, because it's embedded incorrectly.

Charlotte Mew describes the bride as a "leveret", this suggests that...

Grammatically, this is inaccurate.

When used in the above example, "this" signals the beginning of a second independent clause and so the comma should be replaced with either a semi-colon or full stop.

Charlotte Mew describes the bride as a "leveret." This suggests that...

Charlotte Mew describes the bride as a "leveret"; this suggests that...

A third alternative is to use the word "which" as this conjunction demonstrates a relationship between the two clauses:

Charlotte Mew describes the bride as a "leveret", which suggests that...

QUICK QUIZ
1. What is comma splicing?
2. What punctuation should a comma splice *often* be replaced by?
3. What phrasing can solve a comma splice?
4. The following are examples of comma splicing. Rewrite them in two different ways to resolve the splicing.
   a. Sheers writes that his love is like "swans", this extended metaphor shows their love is never-ending.
   b. Hardy describes standing by the "pond", it is clear that the water is stagnant like their relationship.

Writing conclusions

A conclusion needs to summarise your main ideas.

Don't:

- Include anything new.
- Analyse language.
- Repeat yourself.

Do:

- Compare the overall tone or idea of the poems .
- Refer back to the wording of the question.

For example:

For both poets, the sight of a photograph sparks a strong memory that enables them to reflect on their relationship with their parents. While Causley finds comfort and peace in his parents' memory and is drawn towards them, Duffy seems to regret the apparent changes in her mother's life and almost resent the fact that she now seems, as a mother, to be a completely different person.

A 3-sentence conclusion is ideal:

1. What they have in common thematically, using the language of the question.
2. The final overall impression, purpose, or tone of the named poem.
3. The final overall impression, purpose, or tone of the second poem.

Conclusions often sound quite similar in tone or style to introductions – that's fine, because it shows you've stayed on track. However, don't repeat the same phrasing.

QUICK QUIZ:
1. What should you do in a conclusion?
2. What should you avoid doing?
3. What three sentences could you use in a poetry essay conclusion?

How to structure the perfect paragraph

Ok, so there's no perfect paragraph, sorry.

But there is a great way to make you sound more confident and to ensure you get the level of detail you need to.

You might be familiar with some of the following structures or mnemonics:

PEE: Point – Evidence – Explain

PEA: Point – Evidence – Analysis

PETAL Point – Evidence – Technique – Analysis – Link

WETRATS: Writer – Evidence – Technique –Reader – Analysis –   Tone -Structure

WHW: What – How- Why

PEZZ: Point – Evidence – Zoom in – Zoom out

These all have good points if you need something to help you remember what to write about. But they can get a bit formulaic – sometimes they make your writing a bit dull because it feels repetitive to read.

They all have some things in common which are important:
- There's an idea
- They want you to quote
- They remind you to analyse the language

To get a higher grade, looking for patterns of language is better than looking at a single quotation in a paragraph, which is what the above structures sometimes lead to. Patterns helps you to look at those overall themes and ideas that are crucial for Level 4+

Let's break this down a bit more.

What's the point or argument?

Each paragraph needs a topic sentence that tells your examiner what you're writing about right now.

A good structure for this can be:

Writer - Technique – Purpose – Explore

for example:

Sheers [writer] uses the extended metaphor of the swans [technique] to represent the connection between the couple [purpose], exploring whether they too mate for life. [explore]

This can feel you've covered everything already! But in fact it starts you with a broad idea – here, the metaphor of the swans – and then you drill down into examples and range through the poem to explore how this works.

Quotation – Exploration

For the above example, you might use some of the quotations about the swans:

Righting in rough weather	halved themselves
Porcelain	they mate for life
pair of wings settling after flight	icebergs of white feather

You can work through these quotations then, exploring the individual phrases, for example the breakable and fragile nature of the "porcelain" and whether that reflects the couple themselves.

To get a higher grade, try to cluster these quotations further – connect them in different ways.

For the quotations above you might look first at how the swans/couple are described as being fragile, and then secondly at the quotations that suggest they are strong and enduring.

You could also look at whether the tone of the quotations changes – so structurally, you'll be able to see what changes in the relationship.

This is also a great revision technique because you can choose your paragraph topic sentences and cluster the quotations around them e.g.

Charlotte Mew uses the seasons to show her farmer's despair at the passage of time, exploring the breakdown of the relationship.

Berries redden up to Christmastime

More to do at harvest-time

Three summers since I chose a maid.

What do I explore?

- What tone or mood does the quotation suggest?
- Is it the same as the previous one you've chosen or different? Why?
- What alternative reading is there?
- Does this link with the poem's context?
- Is there another example of this somewhere else?
- What does it tell us about the character's feelings or the story of the poem?
- What does it tell us about the writer's attitude to love?

Here's a checklist for a good paragraph:

- ✓ Topic sentence focused on the writer's purpose
- ✓ Several micro-quotations all connected with the topic sentence
- ✓ Key terminology applied correctly
- ✓ Discussion of the writer's purpose as seen through the quotations chosen
- ✓ Repetition of the writer's name (because it helps you focus on the poem as something being created)

Velcro your argument

The last point here is something quite complex – but very effective. It really gets easier if you plan your essay first, too!

A Level 6 essay – grade 8+ – needs to feel like a solid, cohesive argument. Every paragraph should feel like it's in the right place. You shouldn't be able to just rearrange them without feeling like it's no longer working as a cohesive argument.

I use "Velcro paragraphs" to refer to the way they end up hooked together. Think of the last line of the first paragraph as the little hook, and the first line of the next paragraph as the loop that it links into – so they're hard to pull apart.

The following have the connecting ideas underlined.

Last line: The frequent references to "silence" might also be a criticism, suggesting that <u>his behaviour is the more dignified</u> of the two for maintaining a silence around their relationship rather than publicly expressing his unhappiness.

First line: Hardy, too, appears to describe some disgust with <u>his former lover's behaviour.</u>

Last line: Continuing through the poem, <u>the free verse establishes the feel and</u> rhythm of climbing – fluid between movements, occasionally pausing for breath or reflection – <u>and comparing it with the process of understanding.</u>

First line: <u>Heaney's structure also reflects his relationship</u> with his father.

Both these "loop" sentences are quite flexible – the first picks up on the idea of the lover's behaviour, the second on the structure being used. But the idea is that because in the first example, the 'idea' of both is about behaviour, and so they feel like they should belong together.

Using connectives and comparisons like "also", "too," "as well", or "is more romantic" can also help a sense of cohesion.

When you start planning your essays you might find it easy to work in short paragraph pairs to help you create some Velcro.

REVISION TASKS:

Choose a poetry pairing.

Write a series of topic sentences using the write-technique-purpose-explore structure.

Write last / first lines for paragraphs that you could use to Velcro them together.

QUICK QUIZ
1. What are the three ideas in all the paragraph mnemonics?
2. What is a good structure for a 'point' paragraph?
3. Why is clustering quotations a good idea?
4. What is a 'Velcro' paragraph?
5. How do I create Velcro paragraphs?

Revision Guidance
How to quick-plan

SPEND **5** MINUTES PLANNING YOUR ESSAY AND **40** MINUTES WRITING IT.

This will improve your AO1 marks (written communication, organisation and structure) as well as making you feel more confident.

Having a strong critical argument is essential in achieving a top-level mark. Planning helps to make sure that your argument runs throughout the essay.

Planning will take more than 5 minutes at first, but you'll get a lot quicker the more you practise.

Planning steps:

1. Choose your comparison poem
2. Decide your paragraph topics (3-5)
3. Evidence / analysis notes
4. Introduction
5. Conclusion

> ### Exam tip:
> Your plan **does not** get marked but you can use a full page of the exam booklet to get your plan written quickly.

Here's an example:

Compare how poets present ideas about power in relationships in 'Porphyria's Lover' and one other poem from 'Love and Relationships'.[5]

Choose your poem

Exam tip:
You might find at this point your paragraphs aren't easy to write about – change them if that happens!

You can often do this before the exam – some poems work very well together. Check the wording of the exam question to make sure your choices work for this particular question.

Choose pairs that have something in common but differ in their presentation.

Ideally work by theme or idea rather than technique. If you choose poems that both use metaphors of nature as your main link, the rest will often feel forced or you'll run out of good comparison. If, though, you choose two poems that explore painful romance, you can explore the similar and different ways in which they do it.

Choice: Porphyria's Lover / The Farmer's Bride: both are about relationships that are unequal, which causes pain and tragedy. They're both dramatic monologues and use imagery of the weather / seasons to represent the relationship and speakers' feelings.

3-5 paragraphs

Comparison isn't an assessment objective, so there are two approaches: either compare in the same paragraph or go back and forth between the poems. Both approaches work well – for a top grade, a combination is ideal and will help you to explore similarities and differences.

- Dramatic monologue form – power of the speaker
- Power imbalance – silence of the woman
- Imagery of weather / seasons
- Endings

In the example above, you could write four paragraphs which look at both poems together. Note how broad the paragraph topics are – endings, for example. This means there'll be more space to go deeper in the analysis itself. **Start broad and drill down.**

Once you've chosen your paragraphs number them to make the order flow coherently. For example, the power of the speaker in paragraph 1 leads well onto the silence of the woman in paragraph 2.

Evidence / analysis notes

These need to be brief – you only have five minutes or so! You can tick them off as you write about them, to help to keep you focused. You can expand the paragraph topics slightly.

Dramatic monologue form – power of the speaker

Both represent patriarchal thinking of 19th century despite time difference

Male speaker = male power / perspective

Significance of female writer (Mew)?

----

[5] See the model essays at the end for this essay in full

Different tones – PL angry, controlling, righteous/indignant. Self-justification, but underlying madness through rhythm and rhyme. FB hurt, trying to understand what went wrong. Dialect/italics as way to convey conversational style.

Imagery of weather / seasons

PL – pathetic fallacy opening – danger. "spite", "vex", "tore"
"blaze up" – P changes atmosphere; ambiguous danger

F – seasons changes (Harvest, Christmastime) showing change / despair – symbolism. Associated with colours.

Notice the differences in these when it comes to analysis preparation. The first paragraph, about the form of the dramatic monologue, will also look at techniques across the poem, such as rhyme, rhythm, and dialect. These are all technical ways that the writer creates the voice of the character but don't necessarily need quotations.

In the second paragraph, I've checked that I know a few quotations that I can discuss in more detail. Structure will also be a factor (the changing seasons) but the language choices of the pathetic fallacy (vex, spite, tore) are all words I can explore further.

Introduction

A defining characteristic of a level 6 response is a strong argument. Use your planning to make sure that your introduction sets this up. You should include:

- ✓ Which poems you're writing about
- ✓ A reference to the different contexts of the poems
- ✓ A comment on how both poets approach the theme

The plan for this introduction might be:

PL/FB – different ends of the 19th century – patriarchal society's privilege of the male perspective; both in control and it destroys (P – in FB it risks destroying) their relationship.

Conclusion

Use the 3-sentence conclusion style to make sure that you:

- Don't introduce new material
- Include a final comparison
- Step back and weigh up (evaluate) the poets' message or purpose

You might find that conclusions feel like you're repeating your introduction. There **should** be similarities – it means you haven't drifted off-track! By focusing on the poets' tone, message, or purpose, you should have something different to say.

Don't annotate the poem

Although one poem is printed on the paper, use it to help find evidence for your paragraphs. Fully annotating it *then* planning is a waste of time.

You can number quotations on the poem if you find it helpful rather than re-writing them onto your plan.

REVISION TASK:

Use the practice questions on the next pages to write essay plans, one for each poem.

Quick Quiz.

1. What are the 5 steps of planning?
2. How do you choose a good poem?
3. How do you compare the poems in the paragraphs?
4. Where can you write the plan in the exam?

GCSE Example Questions

1. Compare how poets present ideas about the past in 'Before You Were Mine' and one other poem from 'Love and Relationships'.

2. Compare how poets present ideas about memory in 'Before You Were Mine' and one other poem from 'Love and Relationships'.

3. Compare how poets present positive experiences in relationships in 'Climbing My Grandfather' and one other poem from 'Love and Relationships'.

4. Compare how poets present the importance of understanding one another in 'Climbing My Grandfather and one other poem from 'Love and Relationships'.

5. Compare how poets present ideas about looking back on relationships in 'Eden Rock' and one other poem from 'Love and Relationships'.

6. Compare how poets present ideas about relationships between parents and children in 'Eden Rock' and one other poem from 'Love and Relationships'.

7. Compare how poets present ideas about being hurt or damaged in relationships in 'The Farmer's Bride' and one other poem from 'Love and Relationships'.

8. Compare how poets present ideas about the past in 'Follower and one other poem from 'Love and Relationships'.

9. Compare how poets present ideas about changing relationships in 'Follower' and one other poem from 'Love and Relationships'.

10. Compare how poets present ideas about the importance of communication in 'Letters from Yorkshire' and one other poem from 'Love and Relationships'.

11. Compare how poets present ideas about love and nature in 'Letters from Yorkshire' and one other poem from 'Love and Relationships'.

12. Compare how poets present ideas about romantic relationships in 'Love's Philosophy' and one other poem from 'Love and Relationships'.

13. Compare how poets present ideas about new relationships in 'Love's Philosophy' and one other poem from 'Love and Relationships'.

14. Compare how poets present ideas about changing relationships in 'Mother, Any Distance' and one other poem from 'Love and Relationships'.

15. Compare how poets present ideas about relationships with parents in 'Mother, Any Distance' and one other poem from 'Love and Relationships'.

16. Compare how poets present ideas about the end of relationships in 'Neutral Tones' and one other poem from 'Love and Relationships'.

17. Compare how poets present ideas about unhappy experiences of love in 'Neutral Tones' and one other poem from 'Love and Relationships'.

18. Compare how poets present attitudes towards love in 'Porphyria's Lover' and one other poem from 'Love and Relationships'.

19. Compare how poets present ideas about power in relationships in 'Porphyria's Lover' and one other poem from 'Love and Relationships'.

20. Compare how poets present ideas about romantic relationships in 'Singh Song!' and one other poem from 'Love and Relationships'.

21. Compare how poets present ideas about relationships being misunderstood in 'Singh Song!' and one other poem from 'Love and Relationships'.

22. Compare how poets present ideas about obsessive relationships in 'Sonnet 29' and one other poem from 'Love and Relationships'.

23. Compare how poets present ideas about distance in relationships in 'Sonnet 29' and one other poem from 'Love and Relationships'.

24. Compare how poets present ideas about turning points in relationships in 'Walking Away' and one other poem from 'Love and Relationships'.

25. Compare how poets present ideas about relationships between parents and children in 'Walking Away' and one other poem from 'Love and Relationships'.

26. Compare how poets present ideas about the breakdown of relationships in 'When We Two Parted' and one other poem from 'Love and Relationships'.

27. Compare how poets present ideas about painful relationships in 'When We Two Parted' and one other poem from 'Love and Relationships'.

28. Compare how poets present ideas about relationships in difficulty in 'Winter Swans' and one other poem from 'Love and Relationships'.

29. Compare how poets present ideas about close relationships in 'Winter Swans' and one other poem from 'Love and Relationships

How to select quotations to learn

Use your class work and essays

Go back through them and re-read. What quotations did you use often, or write well about?

Learn the beginning and end

The opening and closing lines can tell you a lot about the themes, as well as what changes in the poem which can be a great structural point

Learn clusters of individual words around a theme

For example words about the swans, or in Singh Song! You could list words to describe the bride. Individual words can be explored just as much as whole sentences – and help you look at patterns.

Distil the poem

Select one word from each line of the poem.

Learn what to write as well as quotations - the best quotations will have several comments you can make, including having some good language analysis. The right quotations can make all the difference! It's much harder, for example, to get plenty out of "with a sweet emotion" in Love's Philosophy than the first two lines about the water flowing into one.

You don't need to learn the whole poem off by heart, but you will need to have a very good working knowledge of the poems.

If I was only going to learn two quotes from each poem, these would be my choices:

When We Two Parted	Half-broken hearted	Pale grew thy cheek, and cold
Love's Philosophy	The fountains mingle with the river, and the rivers with the ocean	The sunlight clasps the earth
Porphyria's Lover	She was mine, mine, fair, perfectly pure and good	The sullen wind…tore the elm-tops down for spite
Sonnet 29	My thoughts do twine and bud about thee, as wild vines	Burst, shattered, everywhere!
Neutral Tones	The sun was white as though chidden of God	Alive enough to have strength to die
Letters from Yorkshire	Heartful of headlines Dig and sow	Pouring air and light into an envelope
The Farmer's Bride	She turned afraid of love and me and all things human	The soft young down of her, the brown/the brown of her – her eyes, her hair, her hair!
Walking Away	Like a satellite / wrenched from its orbit, go drifting away	A half-fledged thing set free…who finds no path where the path should be.
Eden Rock	The sky whitens as if lit by three suns	They beckon to me from the other bank
Follower	An expert.	It is my father who keeps stumbling/ behind me, and will not go away.
Mother, any distance	Anchor. Kite	I reach/towards a hatch that opens on an endless sky /to fall or fly
Before you were Mine	Marilyn.	Stamping stars from the wrong pavement
Winter Swans	The waterlogged earth gulping for breath	"They mate for life", you said…I didn't reply
Singh Song!	After vee hav made luv/like vee rowing through Putney	Is priceless baby
Climbing My Grandfather	I discover/the glassy ridge of a scar	Gasping for breath I can only lie/watching clouds and birds circle

How to revise

As we said at the beginning, poetry is simple in some ways because you always know what the questions will be. There are fifteen poems, and the questions will be about the presentation of the relationship.

THINGS YOU WILL NEED TO LEARN:

- The structure of a good essay.
- How to analyse language, structure and form (good analytical writing).
- Key quotations to evidence your points for each poem.
- Relevant structure, form and context for each poem

Those divide into two things;

1. Knowing the poems.
2. Knowing how to write about them – this is covered in the Academic Writing section.

PREPARING TO REVISE THE POEMS

For each poem, make a flash card which includes:

- The structure and form
- Key context
- Several quotations

Preparing to revise the essays

Put the poems into pairs that work well and plan the essay you could write.

Either write the essay and then turn it into a plan that you can learn or use the quick-planning methods from earlier. This means that you can learn the specific essay plan, rather than simply the poems – so that when the question is on, say, Sonnet 29, you know exactly what you'll write about.[6]

REVISION METHODS:

Revision is hard work, but it is worthwhile.

Revision is the way that you essentially put information into your long-term memory and for that to happen, the brain must recognise that it is important. That means making your brain work hard so that it accepts this is something to remember.

---

[6] A note of caution! Do remember to look at the wording of the question. It's extremely likely that a Sonnet 29 question will be on romantic relationships, but it could be phrased as "passionate relationships", "romantic relationships", "relationships with lovers at a distance." In your essay, make sure that you use the wording of the question regularly.

Some useful revision techniques are listed below:

Visualise or use dual coding: Think of an image associated with the quotation or idea – sketch this (quickly! Don't procrastinate with artwork) to remind you. Then link the different images together in a single scene to connect the quotations across the poem.

Flashcards: Put the name of the poem on the front, the 3 sections (structure/form; context; quotations) on the back and ask someone to quiz you.

When you're not using them, stick them where you see them regularly – take over the fridge door or the bathroom mirror!

Write introductions or paragraphs and ask for feedback – writing the whole essay is great too, but it's just as important to focus on the quality of your writing.

Mind-map the quotations and challenge yourself to fill as much of a page as you can with commentary, analysis and links.

Record your essay plans or quotations onto your mobile and listen to them regularly.

Set a five-minute timer and write a plan focusing on one question – how much of the paper can you fill?

Annotate a blank copy of the poem as quickly as you can.

How to use flashcards

Look – cover – write – check
Look at the card, flip it over, recreate it on another piece of paper, check the bits you missed. Write in the bits you missed in a different colour or capitals to remind yourself again. Repeat and repeat.

Don't just do the ones you're confident with! When you're confident, put them to the back of the pile and do the less-confident ones first and spend more time on them.

Ask someone to quiz you
Get them to mix up questions – "Give me a quote from Mother, Any Distance", "What is the context for Sonnet 29?"

Make a Quizlet or Memrise set and play their interactive games.
Ten minutes on the bus or waiting for someone can be spent quizzing yourself

Who's in the bag?
Play games like this with friends who are revising. Put them all in a bag:

Round 1: like Taboo, you can describe the quote without using any of the words in the quote. Work your way through all your cards and put them back in the bag.
Round 2: act out the quotation (easier because you already know what's in the pile!)
Round 3: You get to say just one word to prompt your team to guess the quote (not from the quote itself!)

Learn the front and back

Work in both directions – make sure that you are genuinely recalling the **whole** card before you decide you've learned it.

Use the Leitner method

This is great to make sure you're focused on the ones you find more difficult.

- Have three boxes, labelled 1, 2, and 3.
- Box 1 are the ones you often make mistakes with, Box 3 you get right pretty much all the time, Box 2 is in the middle.
- Study Box 1 more often – and when you get the card right, promote it to Box 2.
- Study Box 2 less often - and when you get the card right, promote it to Box 2. If you get it wrong, demote it to Box 1.
- Study Box 3 to keep it in mind, but less often. If you get a card wrong, demote it to Box 2.

A typical schedule might be studying Box 1 every day, Box 2 every 3 days and Boxy 3 every 5 days.

You could either section off your boxes – or just put all your subjects' flashcards into the three boxes. This would be great for keeping your brain active on all subjects all the time.

There's a good video description of it here:

https://youtu.be/C20EvKtdJwQ

QUICK QUIZ:
1. What are the two parts of revision?
2. List 3 good revision strategies.
3. What are 3 good ways to use flashcards?

What place does this have in a guide to poetry?

I think this might be one of the most important sections.

Revision is hard work. Improving your writing is hard work. And you have a lot of demands on your time. So it's really important to keep in mind what you are doing this for.

Visualising your future goals and your future self can be really useful to keep you motivated.[7]

Spend a few minutes quietly, by yourself, thinking about the reasons you want to do well. You might find it helpful to write them down in a mind-map but it's ok to just think about it if that works for you.

- What grade do you want and why?
- Where will it get you?
- What do you need it for?
- What will it feel like on results day to open that envelope?

Knowing what you want and what steps you're taking to get there is helpful because when you're stuck on something or would rather spend an hour on Netflix instead of revising poetry flashcards, you need something to remind you of why you're doing it.

Watching Netflix for an hour might feel good in the moment. It's comfortable, fun and enjoyable. Revising is hard and, if you're doing it right, uncomfortable because you're trying to learn things and getting them wrong at first.[8] So motivation's really important.

The most successful people are the ones who can delay gratification, and the ones who can see why they're doing what they're doing.

Find your own personal motivation. Make sure you're genuine about it (your subconscious knows when it's being lied to!)

Trying to get a good grade should really be about you and your dreams – but sometimes it's also to impress or please others, like friends, teachers and parents. Try to separate that. It's ok to visualise these people being proud of you but try to think more about what it will mean for you to do well.

If you love English and want to study it later, that's great motivation. But if you don't. remember that most schools, colleges, apprenticeship schemes and universities have entry requirements, for example. Even if they're grade 5 in English, having a higher grade puts you in a better position. Being able to write really well – fluently, academically, persuasively – is useful in your future studies and career. Even very practical trade professions have to write regularly to communicate with clients and suppliers.

For super-charged motivation, try writing your goals down on a notecard and read it regularly to "top up" your subconscious attitude towards your studies.

There are some examples here:

I want to get 5 grade 4s including English and Maths so I can do a painting and decorating apprenticeship. I like doing active things and making things look better, like they're cared for. I think I might like to own my own business one day so English and Maths will help me find good customers and make money.

---

[7] I've written a series of blogs about revising for exams here: http://charlotteunsworth.com/?p=2579
Have a read for more detail.

[8] This is also why you should focus your revision on the things you find hard, not what you find comfortable.

I want to get 8 grade 7s and above, so that I can get into Lansdowne college and do Art, Theatre Studies and Textile Design. I'd love to have a job in the future where I make things, because I love being creative with materials, but I know I need a good set of qualifications to get me going in the right direction. It might be hard, but I can do it.

Model Essays

One of the best ways to improve writing is to read it. Read these essays slowly, thinking about how they structure their introduction, paragraphs, conclusions and how they connect their ideas together.

Read over and over sentences that you like the sound of and practise writing something similar about different poems. This will help your style.

If there are words you don't know, look them up.

Look at the range of interpretive vocabulary as well as the literary / technical vocabulary.

REVISION TASK:

Read the model essays on the next pages.

- Identify literary and interpretive vocabulary.
- Look at the paragraph structures, including the topic sentences and Velcro techniques.
- Look at the balance of poems across the essay.
- Identify historical, thematic and literary context, and think about how much there is and where it comes in.
- Look at the methods of clustering quotations and other ways of exploring evidence like form and structure, which don't always need quotations.

Contents

Compare how poets present unconventional relationships in 'When We Two Parted' and 'Neutral Tones'

For Byron and Hardy, love is misery. With their own turbulent romantic lives and their literary focus on the downtrodden and miserable, it is no surprise that these romance poems also explore the unending, heart-breaking, soul-destroying side of love.

On a first reading, Byron's poem appears to be desolate at the end of a relationship so painful he might be describing a lover's death. Indeed, he uses this semantic field – "sunk chill", "pale grew thy cheek", "sever", "knell" – to create an impression of gothic death as the lover's body turns cold. The refrain "silence and tears" is a mournful, plaintive cry of loss and mourning as he "grieve[s]." Hardy, too, uses language connoting death to describe the end of a relationship he recollects. He personifies the very ground as "starving sod", suggesting that the relationship took a long and painful time to end. He also describes the lover's smile as "the deadest thing / alive enough to have strength to die," conjuring a gruesome, macabre impression of a half-dead thing, briefly reviving only enough to be able to understand its fate, indicative of the way the relationship appeared to be reviving but could not be resuscitated. It also reminds us as readers of relationships that we privately knew to be over, but persisted with anyway with a sort of grim, hopeless determination. Byron's poem seems gentle in comparison.

Hardy's setting echoes the deadened nature of the relationship; the leaves are "grey", rotting on the ground where they have fallen. The sun is "white", a subversion of the usual association of sunlight with happiness; instead, this sun is fading and losing its power to heal. By the end of the poem it is "God-curst", as Hardy sees the 'curse' on everything around him in true pathetic fallacy. Even the water bespeaks the stagnation of the relationship – the "pond" has no current, no change, and no life within it. In contrast, Byron – perhaps unusually for a Romantic poet – does not evoke a sense of setting or the natural world. Instead, his focus is entirely on the other partner in the relationship and the way they have abandoned him.

There is a sense of bitterness in Byron's description with his use of the words "shame", "deceive", "rue" and "broken". The pain of the separation is intense and seems to place the majority of the blame on the partner. Although he "share[s] in its shame", it is her vows that are broken. The archaic "thy" here creates an impression of a marriage "vow", indicating the original strength of the relationship. However, the provenance of the poem suggests that Byron may be making light of the relationship after all. Apparently written for a lover who left their affair (already married) to have an affair elsewhere, the poem emphasises the modifier "half-broken hearted" through its rhythm, implying that the rest of the poem could be interpreted as mockery – he is not broken-hearted at all. This could be echoed in the rhetorical question in the third stanza, and his comment "long, long shall I rue thee" – after all, regret does not necessarily only follow a committed loving relationship. The supposed adultery is implied in the poem through the broken vows and the "fame" that the lover is now experiencing, as well as the line "in secret we met". The lover's behaviour is, therefore, criticised when Byron states "thy heart could forget/thy spirit deceive" – the blame is placed on the lover for her role in ending the relationship. Perhaps, then, the "long years" until they meet again are more of a hope than a fear. The frequent references to "silence" might also be a criticism, suggesting that his behaviour is the more dignified of the two for maintaining a silence around their relationship rather than publicly expressing his unhappiness.

Hardy, too, appears to describe some disgust with his former lover's behaviour. He describes the "eyes that rove/over tedious riddles solved years ago." The phonetic repetition of "rove/over" echoes the repetitive nature of the arguments they endured, the "tedious" discussions that he thought solved, but which were returned to again and again. By emphasising "rove" at the end of the line, Hardy implies, for a fraction of a second, that there was someone else involved – her eyes 'roving' elsewhere – perhaps giving momentary voice to a long-held suspicion. That the words "played between us to and fro" also sounds perpetually dull and meaningless; he doesn't attach importance to the arguments but instead 'playing' suggests a childish carelessness.

There is, in both poems, a sense of looking back at the relationship and viewing it differently from when the writer was in the midst of it. For Hardy, he has learned that "love deceives" and has "shaped to me/your face", viewing the lover as different now that he knows the ending of the relationship. The alliterative "wrings with wrong" draws out the pain of this process, looking back and seeing the relationship not as experienced in the moment but as tainted by the bitterness of its ending. Whether Byron's "half" is significant or not, a similar bitter dissatisfaction is present in his reflections. The lover is dead to him, while he is left to mourn "in silence and tears", unable even to obtain comfort from those around him because of the secret nature of the relationship.

Both poets express the coldness and loneliness that can follow the ending of a romantic relationship, and their bitterness is also a warning about the destructive qualities of love.

Compare how poets present unconventional relationships in 'Singh Song!' and 'Letters From Yorkshire'

In 'Letters from Yorkshire', Maura Dooley's unconventional relationship takes place at a distance, drawing on her autobiographical experiences of having lived and worked between London and Yorkshire. With significant differences in the lives of herself and her partner, Dooley explores the ways that modern technology can, contrary to popular myth, help bridge the gap between people. 'Singh Song!' also explores the concept of distance, although in this case the gap is more cultural, as Nagra tells the story of a second-generation Indian couple newly-married and navigating their place in British culture alongside pervasive stereotypes.

Although the Indian couple have the stereotypical experience of running the corner shop, Nagra's newly-weds also experience clashes of cultural expectation. The bride is "effing at my mum", an unexpected lack of respect for her background, and wearing a "Tartan sari", symbolic of the blending of the fashions of India and fabric of Scotland, just as second generation British-Indians must decide how far to blend their two heritages. Singh also demonstrates a similarly perhaps surprising lack of respect in continuing to lock the shop and running it poorly, as heard in the italicised reported speech and the refrain "di worst Indian shop/on di whole Indian road", despite his father's instructions "not to hav a break". Instead, Singh prioritises his bride and their time together. The bride's job is also unconventional as she is "netting two cats on her Sikh lover site", using online dating technology to make her money – maybe more successfully than her husband.

The couple in 'Letters from Yorkshire' are less physically close than those in 'Singh Song!' as they have chosen, temporarily at least, to live apart while Maura works in London. However, the communication between them maintains their emotional closeness. At the start of the poem, they are communicating through letters: the partner is inspired to "write to me, his knuckles singing", conveying to Dooley the sight of the lapwings returning. This itself is symbolic of the hopeful return of spring, the warmth of their relationship renewing itself again. Further into the poem, Dooley's imagery continues with its romantic connotations. He is "pouring air and light into an envelope" while their "souls tap out messages across the icy miles." The optimistic "air and light" is nurturing, beautiful and calm; although the "icy miles" are between them the distance is being overcome by the strength of their communication.

Each poet explores a narrator who is dominated by their thoughts of someone else. The speaker in 'Singh Song!' neglects his responsibility to the family and their business in his ardour for his new wife. He focuses on her physicality, including her "tummy ov a teddy" and the "eyes of a gun", the unexpected juxtaposition of these two images suggestive of the attraction his wife inspires through her unconventional nature. She is also not conventionally feminine, which is also perhaps a challenge to Indian stereotypes; in addition to the sari she wears a "donkey jacket" and "crew-cut", which portray her as being more dominant in the relationship. By the end, his devotion to her is clear in his romanticised imagery. Just as Dooley romanticises the prosaic nature of technology by imagining their souls communicating through its wires, Nagra portrays the couple in an unexpectedly romanticised location. The description of "silver stool" and "di brightey moon" are suggestive of luxury, as their setting is transformed by their romance. Yet Nagra is also slightly making fun of his couple, as the view of the "beaches of di UK in di brightey moon" is nothing but a poster on the wall.

Dooley's thoughts are similarly dominated by her partner. His letters, while reminding her of home, also feel faintly critical of her choice of occupation. She asks rhetorically, "is your life more real because you dig and sow?", seemingly an echo of a conversation they have had before. She describes the "blank screen", which could sound bitter about the lack of purpose in her work, conveying the news to people rather than making or creating something of her own. However, she refutes this suggestion in favour of the balance between them. She describes the "heartful of headlines", the alliteration lingering over the words and making them sound almost like a caress. She is just as nurturing as him, "feeding words onto a blank screen," and nourishing her work. It is also ultimately her work that brings them together at the end as they are "watching the same news in different houses", finding a sense of connection in doing the same activity even though they cannot be physically together.

Both poets put their couples together at the end of the poem, to highlight the intimacy of the relationship. The Singhs are literally together, physically in the shop with its impressionistic romance, while Maura Dooley and her partner are emotionally, even spiritually, connected through their close communication.

Compare how poets present romantic relationships in 'Love's Philosophy' and 'Sonnet 29'

Percy Shelley uses traditionally Romantic natural imagery to conjure an impression of a world coupled up, blissful in its togetherness, with the final persuasive implication that, therefore, the listener should also want to be a part of this happy pairing. Barrett-Browning's poem is less happy, more questioning of her lover and determined to convince them that she is always thinking of them, as though answering an unheard accusation of forgetfulness.

Shelley's natural imagery creates a progressive sense of coming together. Verbs like "mingle", "mix", "kiss" and "clasp" are all sweet, gentle, even elegant, creating an impression of a caring and nurturing - and natural – relationship. He describes the inevitable increasing in size of the natural elements ("fountains", "river", "ocean", all flowing together), echoing the longed-for relationship increasing in affection until it inevitably consumes the whole of their world. Barrett-Browning explores a similar togetherness through her natural imagery. Her opening line, "I think of thee!" is almost indignant, as though she has been accused of not doing so and is determined to prove herself. As this sonnet formed part of a series of private letters to Robert Browning during their courtship while she was an invalid and they were apart, it's possible this is a response to a question from him about whether she thinks about him and misses him. Her description of the "wild vines about a tree" also reflects a partnership, but there are unsettling undertones. Although her "thoughts do twine and bud", the description of entanglement is surprisingly physical. There are also connotations not of equality, but weakness. The "vine" needs the tree to climb, and potentially for survival, feeding from it. It also perhaps implies that there is a threat of suffocation as there is "nought to see/except the straggling green which hides the wood", implying an underlying fear that the vines – her – will eventually overpower the tree – him – and destroy the relationship.

In both poems, the natural imagery progressively intensifies. Shelley's elements grow in size, the mountains stretching up to heaven, the ocean being formed, heaven and earth finally joining together as the "moonbeams kiss the sea." This anticipates the growth of affection and love between the couple, elevating it to a universal status. Barrett-Browning's intensity, however, is almost painful at times, but also has sexual connotations. As she implores him to "renew thy presence," the pace increases to a breathlessness which culminates in the climactic "burst, shattered, everywhere!" This triad, separated by caesura, echoes the intensity of sexual feeling she imagines, followed by the "deep joy" of peace. The final line echoes the first clause, a return to the impetus for the poem that creates a sense of closure, or fulfilment.

Shelley's final line is likewise the culmination of his argument. His rhetorical question leads to a now all-but-inevitable answer. If the world is naturally paired together, for the listener to reject him would therefore be unnatural, even cruel. It's telling that Shelley doesn't use any aggressive or powerful living images in his poem – he doesn't use animals or the fourth element of fire to convey his ideas; the closest he comes is the intensity of sunlight yet it simply "clasps" the earth. To be overly aggressive would weaken his syllogism[9]. The elements themselves are paired into masculine and feminine, according to the classical categories. In the first stanza, air and water, the feminine, are explored. Then, in a perfect balancing act the second stanza uses earth and light, the masculine. Shelley's rhyming, too, uses a combination of masculine and feminine rhymes. This, however, is not perfectly balanced, but becomes slightly more masculine towards the end ("earth"/"worth", "sea"/"me") as the final persuasion intensifies and his desire to control the outcome increases.

While Shelley becomes (slightly) more intense towards the end as he heightens his persuasion, Barrett-Browning's final lines feel like a settling back, a release or relaxing after the intensity of the exclamation, or sexual expression. She writes using a Petrarchan sonnet form, positioning her poem as a traditional expression of love but also confining her love and passion in the regularity of its formal expectations. Conforming to external restraints,

---

[9] "Syllogism" – a logical argument drawing a conclusion. In Shelley's case, everything in nature is coupled together so it would be natural for us to do the same.

however, allows her vocabulary more freedom to express the bounds of her passion, almost as though she is within a safe space – the privacy of her letters to her lover – but still (just) within the bounds of propriety, as a Victorian woman must be. Barrett-Browning's experience of love is also a deeply disruptive force, echoing the way many Victorian women must have felt. Having been told all their lives to err towards restraint, denying passion, to fall deeply and passionately in love is a dramatic and intense moment. Her natural imagery has echoes of the Bible's 'Song of Solomon', using religious allusion to legitimise her feelings – the reference to the "palm-tree" and the use of the tree/vine feeding from one another. As Shelley uses his rhymes to become more persuasive, Barrett-Browning uses rhythm to become more forceful. In addition to the imperatives "renew", "rustle", "set thy trunk", line 11 changes the rhythm, dropping momentarily out of the confines of the sonnet into a joyful passion with her lover.

Shelley's pastoral poem with its persuasive tone makes love seem natural and inevitable, in a tradition of poems of this kind, contrary to contemporary social restraints which are unnaturally constructed. Given Shelley's advocacy for free love and his scandalous sexual behaviour at the time, however, the natural freedom he is describing could be more self-serving, as the images point to the idea of union and the passion that Barrett-Browning describes, but not marriage. Both poets challenge contemporary expectations of romance governed by restraint yet, in part because of its directed nature and its passionate language, Barrett-Browning's feels the more genuinely in love.

Compare how poets present passionate relationships in 'Porphyria's Lover' and 'Sonnet 29'.

Robert Browning and Elizabeth Barrett Browning both present their speaker's relationships as extremely passionate, to the point of obsession. Browning's poem explores the madness of an unequal relationship and a patriarchal society which expects women to be, impossibly, both chaste and objects of lust. Barrett Browning's, written as part of a series of love letters to Browning during their courtship (and therefore, initially at least, private) is perhaps surprisingly open about her sexual passion considering the era and her status as an unmarried woman.

Both writers use metaphors of nature to explore the feelings of their speakers. For Porphyria's lover, the initial pathetic fallacy creates a violent, aggressive – and miserable – atmosphere. The lexical choices of "vex", "break", "sullen" and "spite" use plosive sounds and sibilance to create harsh, dull sounds – the closed syllables have an aural 'deadness' to them which also contributes to the darkness of the opening lines. Porphyria's entrance is an early turning point as she "made the cheerless grate blaze up", bringing warmth and light literally into his home. However, the verb "blaze" also has connotations of violence and uncontrollability which continues the unsettled atmosphere. The storm also continues outside, implying that the inside of the cottage might be a protected space, but that the couple can't maintain their relationship in the harsh environment of the society outside their door.

Barrett Browning's poem has a calmer and gentler initial use of nature as the "wild vines" entangle themselves around the tree. He symbolism becomes more complex, however. As an invalid much of her life this could be a reference to her feeling as though she relies on the 'strength' of Browning, symbolised through the trunk of the tree, but there is an underlying anxiety surrounding the way that the "straggling green…hides the wood" as though she worries that she is too needy, suffocating her lover even from a distance. As the sonnet continues, her passion builds to a climax: "down – burst, shattered, everywhere!" Structurally, the caesura followed by the exclamatory triplet exudes passion and lust, with its choice of virile, masculine language perhaps being read as a euphemism for ejaculation, though for modern readers this seems a shocking idea considering the modern perception of 'Victorian woman' and her possibilities for self-expression.

Female expression is also at the heart of 'Porphyria's Lover'. The lover's obsession focuses on her physicality, from the removal of the gloves and "let the damp hair fall", both deeply sexualised symbols at the end of the Romantic era. Browning describes Porphyria as active, using dynamic verb choices and focusing on her impact on the room around her: Porphyria "made my cheek lie there"; she is the one to instigate the relationship by coming to the cottage; she "put [his] arm about her waist." In contrast, the lover remains silent and passive at first. Even the decision to kill her is portrayed through passive language as he "found a thing to do". This passivity echoes throughout the poem until the final line: "God has not said a word", which although ambiguous could be read as the speaker seeing approval in God's silence rather than condemnation. It could also, considering Browning's atheism, be a challenge to the contemporary prevalence of Christian belief and be pointing out that there is no God to speak out against the crime. The dramatic monologue forms part of a "Madhouse Cells" collection, with the lover's self-belief seeming to a modern reader to be a version of victim-blaming, an angry rant about Porphyria's femininity and independence – he literally claims that she is "glad [she] has [her] utmost will" at the end, that this is what she wanted. The lover identifies her as being from a higher social class through her gloves, and the reference to "vainer ties" suggests their relationship is illicit, and she is – according to his narrative at least – sexually provocative. The lover also sounds proud that he has in effect frozen her at the instant before she is able to 'soil' herself and become a fallen woman. Although she will "give herself to me", a euphemistic term for losing her virginity, he murders her before their love can be consummated – keeping her at a moment of utmost purity. Here, too, the final line could be construed as finding approval in God's silence, for saving her from her own lustful self.

Barrett Browning's Sonnet 29 also explores some religious ideas alongside her sexual imagery. The 'palm-tree' has connotations of worship, suggesting an almost idolatrous regard for her lover – which she uses elsewhere in her 'Sonnets from the Portuguese' as in Sonnet 43 she explores the transition of her childhood faith to faith in her lover. The intimacy of the sonnet is also similar to that of Browning's monologue; both Porphyria's lover and the speaker of the sonnet are justifying themselves and their actions. The speaker here responds at the beginning ("I think of thee!") with the exclamation mark seeming to be an indignant or frustrated response to an unheard accusation of negligence. Barrett Browning uses the poem's structure to emphasise the paucity of her imagination compared with the reality of having her lover near. From the volta ("I will not have my thoughts instead of thee") to the final line being a slightly altered echo of the first ("I do not think of thee"), she insists that his reality, his presence, is more important to her than the fantasy.

Browning's speaker seems to be delivering a rational narrative at the beginning of the monologue but the revelation of his madness and obsession explores contemporary obsessions with purity and sin, particularly related to young women's sexuality. The lover would rather preserve Porphyria at this supposedly perfect moment than experience a genuine relationship with her. Contrastingly, Barrett Browning sees the reality of her lover as all-important. Although her imagination of Browning is passionate and lustful, she continues throughout to emphasise that for her, his physical presence is what she desires above all else.

Compare how poets present family relationships in 'Walking Away' and 'Mother, Any Distance'.

'Walking Away' and 'Mother, Any Distance' explore a crucial moment of separation in the relationship between parents and children. Although told from contrasting perspectives (one adult, one child), the poems consider the difficulties parents face in letting their children go, both physically and emotionally.

Armitage's speaker describes the freedom and excitement of someone moving into their own home but is also aware of the tension this might create in his relationship with his mother. He stresses his continuing need for her presence by addressing her directly in the first line and stating he will always need "a second pair of hands" to support him. However, the overarching theme is one of freedom and exploration of an exciting future. Armitage uses a semantic field of physical distance - "acres", "prairies" – to connote the seemingly vast expanses of his new home, symbolising the emotional freedom of leaving the family home and starting his adult life. His expansive imagery continues, using the extended metaphor of space exploration to consider the connection between himself and his mother. "Base", "zero-end" and the "line still feeding out" all represent the increasing distance he's putting between the two of them, but also that there remains a strong bond. Ironically, his use of this imagery reminds us he's the child in the relationship, playing on stereotypes of children longing to be astronauts and playing imaginatively.

Day-Lewis similarly uses space imagery in his poem, reflecting a moment in his son's childhood when the child goes to play with his friends. It's a crucial moment of independence, when the child doesn't look back for permission but simply moves towards his friends. Here, the imagery is less positive as the satellite is "wrenched from its orbit", a harsh violent motion that drags the satellite – the child – away from the gravitational pull of the parent. Day-Lewis positions himself as the guiding (or controlling?) force in his child's life, much as Armitage's mother is the "base" from which he leaves. Yet as Day-Lewis's poem is written from the parent's perspective we see a child helpless and lost, not gaining independence. This impression is further developed through the natural imagery. The child is a "half-fledged thing", half-grown and barely recognisable in the "wilderness". His actions are "hesitant", "eddying" rather than deliberate, representing him as helpless, hopeless and unable to find his way. Although the movements are associated with nature, Day-Lewis seems unable to fully appreciate that the moving on is also natural and must persuade himself of it towards the end of the poem.

Despite the language of separation, the child-speaker of 'Mother, Any Distance' recognises the importance of his mother. She remains "base", and the two of them are "Anchor. Kite." The caesura in this phrase suggests the distance between them, but also functions as a way to join them together – it almost seems to place them more closely side by side than if Armitage had written a conjunction, an additional word wedged between the two of them. Instead, they are nestled against the full stop beside one another. "Anchor" might have negative connotations in some circumstances, such as being held back. But considering the positivity of the rest of the poem it seems here to be optimistic – a cord to remain tethered, enabling the speaker to 'fly' in safety without drifting off into sky and becoming lost (the fate Day-Lewis fears for his child). The final line is also optimistic for his supported future as he will "fall or fly". While Armitage uses a monosyllabic parallelism, he also places the word "fly" at the end of the poem, with its open syllable echoing the possibility the speaker feels for his future.

Contrastingly, Day-Lewis is not optimistic by the end of his poem. He sees "something I never quite grasp" and there's a feeling of resignation, giving himself up to the idea of losing his child. He uses language related to religion ("irresolute clay", "ordeals" and "God") to suggest that there is a plan in the workings of the universe that he must trust without understanding. His final line "Love is proved in the letting go" is a reworking of the idiom "if you love something, set it free," itself quite a clichéd idea that seems to offer him little genuine comfort. He is "letting go" his child in this moment but without feeling happy or confident that his son can find himself. Although he acknowledges "I have had worse partings", he sees these small moments as examples of chipping away at the close father-son relationship, perhaps imperceptible at the time and only understood in hindsight.

Day-Lewis's poem is morose, dwelling on the anxiety parents feel in seeing their children move away from them, and seeing each movement as an inevitable progression towards leaving their parents behind. Contrastingly,

Armitage's speaker might emphasise the physical distance opening between him and his mother, but it is always with a solid understanding that the emotional relationship remains essential, as close as ever.

Compare how poets present distant relationships in 'The Farmer's Bride' and 'Letters from Yorkshire'.

'The Farmer's Bride' and 'Letters from Yorkshire' explore different kinds of distance. The emotional distance between the farmer and his bride in Charlotte Mew's poem represents the misery of a marriage without love or communication. In 'Letters from Yorkshire', communication is crucial in maintaining a relationship that instead suffers from a physical distance.

Mew uses imagery of the seasons to structure her poem, exploring the changes over the course of the relationships. It begins at "harvest-time", traditionally a symbol of fertility and reaping possibility, but here used as a reason for the hasty courtship. The Farmer's comment "more's to do…than bide and woo" reflects his very pragmatic stance, needing the time to commit to his work rather than their relationship. His reflective "maybe" suggests that he might now regret this speed, thinking that the marriage might now be stronger if they had had more time to get to know one another. The "three summers" indicates the passage of time, and the deterioration of their marriage – although "summers" should symbolise warmth and optimism, this is no longer the case as the "short days shorten" and their relationship wanes. The farmer's regretful rhetorical question "what's Christmas-time without there be some other in the house than we?" demonstrates his wistful unhappiness at the lack of children in the marriage, itself an indication of wider problems in the relationship. By measuring the marriage in seasons, Mew emphasises the farmer's relationship with his work and the natural world around him, emphasising the idea that this is how he understands his life – a stark contrast with his later description of his wife.

Dooley also uses natural imagery and the seasons to represent the speaker and her partner. He writes to her in "February" "planting potatoes", an image that suggests preparing a harvest for the future. Unlike the Farmer's harvest/marriage, which is as yet infertile, Dooley's partner seems to be further investing in the future, hopeful that their relationship will continue to improve. He is "breaking ice", "clearing a path", verbs that metaphorically suggest efforts to clear the way in their relationship as well and 'warm up' the physical distance between the two of them. Dooley's pragmatic tone it's "simply how things are" suggest a mature acceptance that, at this stage in their lives, they must be apart physically, but that they can still continue to believe their relationship will survive as long as they continue to communicate.

Dooley describes her couple communicating in romanticised imagery, "pouring light and air into an envelope." The verb "pouring" is expansive and generous, not holding back but creating an impression for her of the love he feels. "Light and air" might be a surprising image, considering the very earthy imagery of the potatoes and waterbutt, but implies her romantic association of the lover and his rural lifestyle in contrast to her own urban existence. She, too, communicates with passionate imagery – a "heartful of headlines" which, although not all directed at him, represent her intense desire to communicate, and she sees her work as reaching him too. Finally, their souls "tap out messages across the icy miles" – although "tapping" might be tentative, it is also, here, continuous (almost like Morse code) and the "icy miles" seem little distance when they are so closely connected.

Mew's couple, however, discover that communication has broken down completely and opened up a physical as well as emotional distance between them. Although the farmer's monologue describes the bride with animalistic imagery, it is wild and untamed. She is a "leveret", "mouse", "mong the sheep", at home more with the wild prey creatures than in the community where she lives. Unlike the farm animals, he cannot understand her, instead seeing her as a "frightened little fay" implying his confusion, seeing her as something other than human, so deep is the rift between them. All he can do is "fetch her home" when she runs away, like a wild animal being chased by the hunt. In the final stanza, the physical distance comes to possess him; he imagines her in the attic room, a "maid". There is not only the physical distance of the staircase between them but the emotional; "maid" has connotations of servant rather than wife, as servants traditionally slept in the attic, indicating that this might be how she sees herself as we presume she has chosen to sleep there. It might also imply that the consummation of their relationship has been, or become, impossible. Yet the agonising closeness of her torments him – "'tis but a stair" – as though he could cross the barrier at any moment. His final repetition, "her eyes, her hair, her hair!" expresses his desperation at the tragedy their marriage has become as well as is frustration and is ambiguous. Is he so overcome he would make his way into the attic? Or simply desperate for love and affection from the woman he has chosen to marry?

Both poets explore the physical and emotional distance that can open up in a relationship, sometimes as a result of a lack of communication. Dooley's speaker struggles with the physical distance but finds comfort in their continuing emotional connection and strong communication. Contrastingly, the Farmer has become increasingly despairing as the emotional distance between him and his bride continues to develop, and the small physical distance of a staircase seems insurmountable.

Compare how poets present the relationship between parents and children in 'Follower' and 'Before You Were Mine'.

In 'Follower', Heaney explores the way that children follow in their parents' metaphorical – and literal – footsteps. Through its extended metaphors, the speaker considers how parents forge a path, shaping the world around them, and the ways that children must then interpret their own movement through the world either re-forging their parents' paths or creating a new one. In 'Before You Were Mine', Carol Ann Duffy also reflects on how children look at their parents. In her poem, Duffy memorialises her mother but acknowledges her understanding is finite: her imagination must fill in the gaps of her mother's life.

Heaney uses the rural natural setting of his upbringing to represent the relationship between speaker and father. With an extended nautical metaphor, Heaney describes his father ploughing the land. This could be interpreted as a symbol of control - trying to shape nature into an organised farmstead – and there is also a strong impression of exploration, of furrowing a path, developing a metaphor for finding a way through the wilderness of life to create a manageable, understandable existence. The father himself is "globed like a full sail" which implies the physical difficulty of bending nature to one's will, the rounded back showing the physical hardships he has faced. This simile suggests the father's force of will, intent on his pursuit, attacking it energetically, borne forward by the 'wind' of his determination. Heaney calls him an "expert", placing the phrase with its full-stopped caesura at the opening of the second stanza. The tone is definitive and admiring, seeing the powerful force of his father's work.

Duffy similarly admires her mother. Using a photograph as the inspiration for her writing, she describes her mother's physical appearance. She uses the allusion to Hollywood actress "Marilyn" Monroe in a way similar to that of Heaney's "an expert", separating the reference at the end of the line. The allusion to the iconic star and the distinction of the character from the two friends in the photograph calls to mind the wider problems Marilyn suffered and the lengths she went to in order to maintain an illusion of happiness in public. This could be seen as Duffy's acknowledgement that she doesn't truly know her mother, certainly not before her own birth, and is having to create, to an extent, her impression of her through imperfect means. The glamourous representation continues as Duffy's imagination takes over from description. She thinks of "fizzy movie tomorrows", "a ballroom with the thousand eyes", her mother the centre of everyone's attention. There is an element of idealisation, too, not only in the Monroe reference but her comment towards the end that she prefers the girl of her imagination, young and carefree before babies and responsibility.

In Heaney's poem, responsibility passes from father to son by the poem's end. The son describes himself "stumb[ling]" behind his father, sometimes even carried – "he rode me on his back". There's also a desire to follow in his father's footsteps metaphorically, to "grow up and plough", even as a young child seeing the physical attributes of his father ("close one eye, stiffen my arm") as qualities to emulate. Yet he also sees himself, in hindsight, as a "nuisance, tripping falling / yapping always". The present-participle verbs sound childish, with the line break emphasising the hesitation in his gait, contrasting with the "dipping and rising" that mimics the rise and fall of the father's walk. Yet this is immediately followed by a volta of sorts;

"but today,
it is my father who keeps stumbling
behind me."

Just as the child fell, the father now follows and falls. In the same way, representing their closeness, Heaney also places this second fall at the end of the line to emphasise the indecision that may now come with age. Again, this is potentially both literal and metaphorical. Literally, it is the father, showing the son the ropes but unable to perform the intense physical action himself. Metaphorically, it is the memory of him, symbolically following the son in every moment he has on the farm his father loved and worked on his whole life.

Contrastingly, Duffy's relationship with her mother doesn't appear to move on and, indeed, is barely a part of the way she views her mother. The speaker appears to see herself, as the son in 'Follower' does, as a nuisance. She comments in a rhetorical question "the decade ahead of my loud, possessive yell was the best one, eh?" The colloquial exclamative "eh" could be sarcastic, indicating resentment from the poet or perhaps recollection of conversations which have left her feeling rejected. It could, alternatively, be a sympathetic tone, as the speaker understands the restrictions that come with a child. The speaker calls herself "possessive", a trait echoed in the very title of the poem 'Before You Were Mine' and there is a demanding tone elsewhere – "I wanted the bold girl winking" – as though the child feels possessive over the mother's whole life, not just their existence since her birth.

Duffy's final images are of the glamour of her mother's previous life, "where you sparkle and waltz and laugh", with the syndetic list apparently endless – until, at least, the child comes along and claims her, changing everything. Heaney's poem ends with a similarly stark contrast between father and son, examining the changes that occur in the parents' lives. Although Heaney seems reflective and keen, still, to learn from his father's example, Duffy's poem is filled with regret that she never knew the girl her mother used to be.

Compare how poets present the ending of relationships in Neutral Tones and Winter Swans.

Neutral Tones and Winter Swans explore the endings of relationships. Thomas Hardy's poem is a bitter reflection on a past relationship and the ongoing pain it can cause. Nearly a century later, Owen Sheers' couple are similarly facing the end of their relationship. The poem is from his collection "Skirrid Hill", "skirrid" being Welsh for "divorce." Although the poem's ending is ambiguous, this provenance implies that the reunion is at best temporary.

Sheers and Hardy both use imagery of water as the central theme to explore the anguish of their relationships. At the opening of Neutral Tones, the speaker reflects: "we stood by a pond that winter day." The stagnant water of the pond, unmoved by currents or tides, is reflected in the cyclical nature of the poem which returns to the image at the end, now with the "pond edged with greyish leaves." Nothing has changed in the relationship; they remain separated, but in pain. Sheers' couple, too, begin beside water albeit initially more disturbed and potentially threatening, as the "waterlogged earth gulped for breath" beside the lake, Personifying the struggling ground represents the conflicts within the relationship, the couple gasping for air despite the suffocation of the "storms" that have raged for two days. Yet Sheers allows some optimism to creep in; there's a "break in which we walked" offering a chance of reconciliation – is it possible that the storms, or arguments, will be amicably resolved? Or is the undertone instead suggesting a more ominous and permanent "break"? Lakes, however, unlike ponds, have currents and move, perhaps indicating that the couple may be able to move on from their trauma.

Both poets also use pathetic fallacy. Hardy's setting of a "winter day" draws attention to the harsh and often difficult season, with its cold weather and the death of nature. The motif of wintry death continues throughout the poem, showing that that the narrator has no hope of the relationship's revival. Hardy couples this with his use of colour imagery, the "grey" fallen leaves contrast with the "white" sun but both are the "neutral tones" of the title. Even the sun is pale as "white" suggests the weakened half-light of mid-December, rather than its usual joyful yellow. Hardy's narrator attempts to distance himself from the relationship by calling them "neutral", but this seems self-deceiving; his despair indicates instead he has become deadened by the experience. The morbid natural imagery continues. The soil itself is "starving", much like the "gasping" "waterlogged" earth in 'Winter Swans', which uses the pathetic fallacy of the season in the title. Contrary to Hardy, though, Sheers focuses more on the momentary calm they are now in.

Both use their poems' forms to convey the speaker's feelings. Sheers, as a modern poet, uses free verse, but his series of three-line stanzas are uneven and disjointed in an echo of the relationship itself. Although resolving into a couplet at the end, he resists the temptation to form a rhyming couplet, instead maintaining a separation between the two lines that contributes to the ambiguity of the ending – there is not a final resolution to the couple's situation although they are temporarily reconciled. Hardy's tightly controlled structure reflects the speakers' tight control of their emotions, perhaps afraid of allowing themselves to feel the loss more deeply. He uses 4 regular quatrains in an ABBA scheme throughout; maybe the relationship itself was passionless, too controlled to be genuine. However, the final line of each stanza feels as though it is rhythmically cut slightly short, as though the speaker must rein himself in to prevent his emotions spilling out.

Ideas about longevity of relationships – of lack thereof – pervade both poems. Hardy develops the morbid tone of the poem through his setting, a world devoid of life: the "ash" tree is dead, the winter surrounding them leaves no hope of the new life of spring. Hardy also uses juxtaposition in the perverse description of his lover's smile, "alive enough to have strength to die", emphasising the final syllable to focus Hardy's pessimism surrounding the futility of the relationship. The paradox of the description of her "bitter" "grin" highlights the underlying confusion and discord within the relationship. Sheers also uses paradox in the extended swan metaphor, describing them as "icebergs of white feather", contrasting the hard and soft, alongside the fragile "porcelain". For the couple in 'Winter Swans', conversation and communication is similarly stilted and difficult. Although we are reminded that they (the swans) "mate for life", the image is both wistful and romantic, full of unspoken question – have we? The speaker's lack of response is telling. Although by the end they are holding hands, the movement seems to be all on the lover's part as the speaker merely "noticed" their joining.

Despite their different eras, both poets recognise the pain that the end of a relationship can cause, while it is in progress and when it is done. Their strikingly similar techniques suggest, perhaps, that human experiences of love and loss has not, after all, changed much in the time between them.

Compare how poets present relationships between parents and children in 'Eden Rock' and 'Before You Were Mine'

The nostalgia of both "Eden Rock" and "Before You Were Mine" centres around the loss of parents, from adult children trying in some way to recapture the certainty of their youth. For Causley, the certainty is in their ever-present nature – he is confident that they are "waiting for me" although he is unsure precisely where. Duffy, on the other hand, appears to be searching for a deeper confirmation of love; she seems to doubt her mother or, at least, want reassurance that the significant changes that took place in her mother's life after her birth didn't lead to her mother's regret.

Causley is confident in his parents' comforting presence even as he appears to contemplate death. The river is a common literary trope of death, whether the rivers of Lethe and Styx in Greek myth, which the dead would have to cross (or the colloquial term 'pass over') to reach the underworld and which would erase their memory of the past. Yet the scene is a peaceful one. The sun is gentle, weather good enough for a picnic and his father is "leisurely" skimming stones – an idyllic setting that implies he looks back on his relationship with his parents with fond, uncomplicated nostalgia. Duffy's setting is more energetic, though also seemingly inspired by a photograph. The girls "shriek at the pavement" on a night out, and "clatter...over George Square," bringing the noise and excitement of youth to the scene. Duffy uses these sounds of enjoyment to contrast with her "possessive yell", a harsher and more aggressive, even upsetting, noise, wondering if this noisy entrance ruined her mother's life. Other senses too provide a memory as Duffy uses synaesthesia ("I see you, clear as scent") to evoke the sense of her mother's ghost, possible drawing parallels with the way that scent provokes some of the strongest memories. Both poets use light frequently; for Duffy, references to streetlights and stars are suggestive of the glamourous life she imagines her mother leading, while Causley's parents are bathed in sunshine, a bright, warm and gentle light that implies their place in a kind of heaven.

Duffy describes her mother with longing but focuses on the time before she was born with a "polka-dot dress", and "high-heeled red shoes" symbolic of dancing, care-free life, and sexually suggestive, though now reduced to child's playthings as Duffy remembers her hands in them. This is echoed in the "small bites on your neck", perhaps a strange physical detail for her daughter to focus on but one which suggests the new sexual freedom discovered in the era and alluded to in the conflict between her mother and grandmother ("Your Ma stands at the close/with a hiding for the late one." This suggestiveness is also perhaps a reflection of Duffy's disappointment in her mother's straighter-laced nature once her daughter is born. Although she teaches her dance steps it's "on the way home from Mass" and the "bold girl" has disappeared. Causley's parents are just as vividly drawn, though more fondly. He remembers them in their youth, his mother associated with an almost faded prettiness characteristic of photographs from the turn of the century, "sprigged dress, "ribbon in her straw hat", "her hair, the colour of wheat, takes on the light". She is associated with the natural world though the light, the wheat, even the fabric of her hat. She's welcoming in her actions, the one to prepare the picnic with "three plates" waiting for her son to join them. Likewise, Causley's father is characteristic of his era, picnicking "in the same suit/of Genuine Irish Tweed", the capitalisation a wry, fond remembrance. The parents are pictured in their heyday, a youthful memory rather than one of age which perhaps reflects Causley's age when writing the poem, looking back at his youth rather than his later life as he approaches death.

The unity of the family is evident throughout. His mother prepares "the same three plates," indicating this is just one example of a common occurrence. Then there are "three suns" in the sky, a weather phenomenon often associated with good omens and which could in this case be interpreted as the universe blessing the family as they are becoming reunited. It also creates the other-worldly sense of a heaven, in which things are slightly different tot our own reality. The only note of disharmony is in Causley's final line. Whereas he has previously used four-line stanzas, this final one is split 3-1, with his last comment ("I had not thought it would be like this") sounding less than certain due to his use of the subjunctive tense. The separation of the final line also suggests his hesitation, reflecting a desire to stay separate from his parents a while longer. Duffy also uses the structure of her poem to reflect change, writing of her mother's life as unfulfilled as she emphasises the changes in her mother's lifestyle. She begins as "Marilyn", the end-stopped line almost breathless in admiration of the way she emulates the Hollywood icon. Yet by the end, she is "stamping stars from the wrong pavement", stuck in Glasgow with her child rather than chasing the American dream of fame and fortune. The final description of her "glamourous love…you sparkle and waltz and laugh" is merely a dream, not even a memory, of the time before Duffy herself was born.

For both poets, the sight of a photograph sparks a strong memory that enables them to reflect on their relationship with their parents. While Causley finds comfort and peace in his parents' memory and is drawn towards them, Duffy seems to regret the apparent changes in her mother's life and almost resent the fact that she now seems, as a mother, to be a completely different person.

Compare how poets present relationships between parents and children in 'Climbing My grandfather' and 'Follower'.

In "Climbing My Grandfather" and "Follower", the speakers explore their relationship with parental figures, with a kind of exploratory nostalgia that reflects the closeness of these relationships, yet also struggles with the distance of generations.

Andrew Waterhouse, as a keen environmentalist and climber himself, uses the extended metaphor of climbing to explore the nature of getting to know someone. Throughout his poem, the language of climbing expresses his struggle. He gets "good purchase" early on, symbolising the things he already knows and can 'hang onto' to help him delve further as he is "trying to get a grip" and understand his grandfather's experiences further. The climbing becomes harder the higher he gets, reflecting the difficulties of building intimate relationships, perhaps especially when the generational divide is so immense as children can't comprehend the lives of those who lived before they were born. By the time he reaches the summit, and has a deeper understanding, he is "gasping for breath [and] can only lie/watching", exhausted by the effort.

Heaney similarly uses natural imagery to explore his father, although in his case the nature is associated with his father's character, depicting him as a force of nature itself. His father controls and understands the natural world as an "expert", able to "map[] the furrow exactly". Heaney uses an extended metaphor of sailing to convey his father's skill, portraying him as an experienced adventurer. The "sod rolled over without breaking" like a wave, as his father is "globed like a full sail strung", as though he himself were a ship on the ocean. This image gives an impression of gliding effortlessly, while acknowledging the realities of the intense effort needed to successfully navigate the seas, and Heaney's father's work.

The form and structure of "Climbing My Grandfather" reflects the struggle; the free verse is wryly acknowledged in the first line ("I decide to do it free, without a rope or net"), another climbing metaphor but also suggesting that the writer is aware that there is no guidance available in building this relationship – he will have to feel his way gently, carefully, and ensure that he takes his time to do it right. Continuing through the poem, the free verse establishes the feel and rhythm of climbing – fluid between movements, occasionally pausing for breath or reflection – and comparing it with the process of understanding.

Heaney's structure also reflects his relationship with his father. The four-line regular stanzas give the appearance of continuity, the farm and its work passing through the generations from father to son – yet they could also be seen as less emotional than Waterhouse's poem. There is less urgency to understand his father, more a sense that he already knows and admires him, as he "wanted to grow up and plough". Yet the past tense in this line suggests that there is also a distance in the poem; this may have been a childhood dream but it's unclear as to whether the speaker is now doing this or not. The contrast between childhood and adulthood is structurally crucial to the poem; the child speaker followed "in his broad shadow", perhaps literally but also metaphorically in his father's shadow, awed by his expertise and unable to live up to him. The verbs associated with the child reflect this feeling of awkward clumsiness ("tripping, falling/yapping"), the speaker remembering how much of a burden he felt. Interestingly, his father doesn't treat him this way instead he "rode me on his back", a kind, loving and typically fatherly gesture, so perhaps the sensation of awkwardness is more present in hindsight. This awkwardness, however, is conferred to the father by the end of the poem as their roles have reversed: "today/it is my father who keeps stumbling/…and will not go away." Again, this could be literal if the son is farming and the father is struggling to keep up as he ages. It could also again be a metaphor for the son feeling as though the father is always behind him, reminding him how to do things and how to live.

Waterhouse also sees some distance in his relationship with his grandfather, although it is less problematic than Heaney's. There are moments when he pauses, particularly in the middle when he finds the "glassy ridge of a scar". The tone changes as he is 'gentle' rather than continuing, moving around the scar instead of investigating it. In climbing, a 'scar' is a bare place on a mountain which could be difficult to hold onto and might be dangerous. This moment is also a reminder of the visual image of a child 'climbing' a sitting adult, scrambling across them – as a literal scar, it could be a war wound or other sign of traumatic injury. Waterhouse sensitively moves over the spot and leaves it behind; he wants to understand his grandfather but not dredge up painful memories.

In both poems, too, the speakers find admiration for their parental figures, though this is more problematic in 'Follower'. Waterhouse ends his poem at the summit of his grandfather-mountain, with the "slow pulse of his good heart". The slow pace echoes the rhythm of a heartbeat, and there is a deep sense of contentment that Waterhouse has achieved his desire to be close, understand his grandfather, as symbolised through the "clouds and birds" of his inner thoughts. Heaney's admiration for his father's expertise is evident throughout, although whether he always feels this expertise to be totally uncritical of him is not quite clear.

Compare how poets present ideas about power in relationships in 'Porphyria's Lover' and one other poem from 'Love and Relationships'

Despite their different genders and writing nearly 80 years apart, Browning and Mew both explore the problematic nature of the patriarchal, unequal society in which they lived. Browning's Lover is obsessive to the point of destruction, driven mad in part by a need to possess a woman who exercises unusual authority for the time and makes him feel powerless. Mew's farmer has disturbing hints, at the end, of a similar obsession, yet Mew's sympathetic portrayal suggests his desperation is borne of a society which insists women marry – and lose much of their freedom in the process – yet also insists men and women can't genuinely know one another before marriage.

Browning's use of the dramatic monologue form positions the male speaker as being in control of the relationship throughout, until his murder of Porphyria. We as readers see only his perspective and must infer the rest from his ranting monologue. However, towards the beginning of the narrative, it is Porphyria who is in control. Browning's verb choices for Porphyria are dynamic – she "made the cheerless grate/blaze up" and she is the one who "sat" beside him, "put my arm about her waist" and "made my cheek lie there." In contrast, the lover is entirely passive, even physically moved by Porphyria in a macabre wax effigy-like mimicry of affection. The lover describes himself as silent and unresponsive despite her efforts, until a shift in understanding occurs when he "knew/Porphyria worshipped me." This elevation of himself to godlike status is consolidated in his wresting power from her. From this moment, his actions become deliberate – he "wound/three times her little throat around", "propped her head up" - directly mirroring Porphyria's actions by placing her head on his shoulder instead. The speaker positions himself as all-powerful yet Browning demonstrates his madness through the regularity of the rhythm and ABABB rhyme scheme. The iambic tetrameter is cheerful and jaunty, but the conflict of this upbeat tone with the horror of the scene at the end makes it even more disturbing while the structured ABABB could suggest that although the speaker is trying to restrain his emotions, they threaten to break free and overwhelm him at any moment.

Mew's Farmer is far less violent but does exhibit the helplessness and obsession that could quickly shift and turn into rage. In crafting a masculine voice through her dramatic monologue, Mew silences her female protagonist, a fact commented on by the farmer: "I've hardly heard her speak at all." His opening statement "I chose a maid" highlights the patriarchal authority with which he speaks, not acknowledging his bride's choice. Although it's unlikely this was a traditionally arranged marriage, given the class and time period of the farmer, there would likely be an economic or social pressure on the bride. Perhaps too late, the farmer acknowledges a lack of consideration in the marriage – "more's to do at harvest-time to bide and woo" – beginning their relationship by putting his work first. The farmer's power is further demonstrated in the social community surrounding the marriage. When the bride runs away, "we caught her, fetched her home at last/and turned the key upon her, fast." The plural pronoun indicates that the community has joined together to return her to her marriage, and condoned – even encouraged – physically locking her in her home to 'tame' her.

The bride's lack of power is demonstrated through her silence not only in denying her a voice in the poem, but in the farmer's depiction of her silence among humans. Although she speaks to "beast in stall" and will "chat and play with birds and rabbits", she will not speak to her husband. This denial is, strangely, more akin to the Lover's refusal to speak at the opening of Porphyria's Lover, a method of claiming power through withdrawal. The imagery associated with the bride continues the power imbalance. She is characterised as a "leveret", "mouse," "hare", a series of wild creatures who are small prey animals – positioning the farmer as the opposite, the predator. This also makes her appear wild and untameable, the "frightened fay" or something otherworldly that the farmer, used to docile tamed animals and a natural world he can work with, can't understand.

Browning's Porphyria is also silent throughout, but her thoughts and opinions are given to us by the lover as though they were fact, as part of his self-justification. Although hardly realistic in some senses - published in a collection called "Madhouse Cells" reflecting the insanity of the speaker - the story of domestic violence is, sadly, all too real. Porphyria's "vainer ties" in society hint at a more powerful social class, while naming her should

71

convey power; names are traditionally important, conveying a specific identity and enabling us as readers to imagine one individual. The possessive "Porphyria's lover should render the other partner as more submissive, less important – valued only for their relationship to the named character. It might be expected that the lover is female, for this reason, privileging the masculine. By inverting this expectation, however, Browning draws attention to Porphyria through her name and yet the poem is titled about her lover, suggesting he is the most significant. By not giving him a name, Browning also makes him a horrifying everyman figure, who could be representative of men's gothic desires to control and manipulate women.

Despite the "lover" title of the poem, Browning's pathetic fallacy in the opening is language of hatred: "vex the lake", "tore the treetops down for spite", a scene of wanton destruction caused through anger and jealousy, foreshadowing Porphyria's murder. The angry description ("vex", "tore", "spite") demonstrate the destructive power of the environment and foreshadow the lover's destruction of her life. Even when she makes the "cheerless grate blaze up," the verb "blaze" is vicious rather than comforting, suggesting destructive power in the cottage. Mew similarly uses pathetic fallacy and imagery of the seasons, to track the deterioration of the farmer's relationship. They marry at "harvest time", traditionally associated with fertility and promise, which is quickly destroyed. The farmer measures their relationship as "three summers", reflecting his concern with the changes in nature through the year that he must work with. Yet the bride changes "like the shut of a winter's day", closing herself away from the farmer. When it reaches winter, the cold greys and blues are despairing and miserable as the farmer contemplates a lack of children in the household: "What's Christmas-time without there be some other in the house than we!"

This lack of children suggests his desire for the typical family life, but also has a darker undertone of potential sexual frustration and expression, which could be seen as coming to a head in the final stanza. Frustrated by the short distance between them, the farmer's repetition ("the soft young down of her…Her eyes, her hair, her hair!") is a pitiful cry of sexual frustration, obsessed with her physicality. It is possible to read the farmer as being early in the process of patriarchal entitlement that drives the Lover to kill. Browning's character portrayal of himself as godlike climaxes at the end when he claims, "god has not said a word!", a defiant and triumphant final statement. This could be a claim that god condones his actions, but given Browning's brief atheism when influenced by Percy Shelley, it is also possible that he is claiming the absence of god and, therefore, the absence of an absolute morality: certainly enough to put him in the 'Madhouse Cells'.

While both writers explore the problems of a power imbalance in a relationship, neither suggest a social cause or way to resolve the inequalities of gender and social class that trouble these characters. Browning's lover is determined to take control at all costs, from Porphryia, the society that keeps them apart, and even god himself. Mew's farmer, more realistic and prosaic, is miserable because the lack of equality in the relationship is exacerbated by their poor communication.

Compare how poets present relationships with parents in Walking Away and Eden Rock

Walking Away, from a parent's perspective, looks back with nostalgia and sadness at a crucial moment in a child's development. Day Lewis remembers this moment as significant in the child turning inevitably away from his father into his adult life. Causley is similarly nostalgic in his poem but, perhaps because it is from the child's perspective, he focuses on the nostalgia felt towards the parents who are now gone and explores his feelings about death.

The poems' titles suggest their attitudes. Walking Away places the focus firmly on the child's actions, and word "away" implies a sense of bereavement or abandonment from the father's perspective. "Walking" is also a slow verb which could suggest a sense of deliberation; although this is contradicted later when the child is "drifting" (far more thoughtless and accidental) it maybe suggests that the father feels the child has deliberately left him. Eden Rock is quite oxymoronic; while "Eden" implies the heaven in which his parents are waiting, "Rock" is an empty, barren place. The contrast of these two words suggests that his view of the afterlife is complex and shifting, that he isn't as certain as the gentle tone of the poem might imply.

Day Lewis uses natural imagery to depict his child as not quite ready to leave his father. He describes the child as a "half-fledged thing", a metaphor for a bird leaving the nest too soon. This uncertainty continues throughout the poem as the figure is "hesitant", "eddying away" rather than walking with confidence. The impression of a child "eddying" suggests that he is borne with the current, which might also be implying that he is too swayed by his peers rather than knowing his own mind and choosing his own path. He is a "winged stem, loosened" from his father and no longer has guidance to keep him safe: most seeds do not take root but die instead.

Told from a child's perspective instead, Causley's poem has a similar nostalgia, but he is far more optimistic about the future relationship between himself and his parents. He imagines them at their best. His father is in "the same suit of Genuine Irish Tweed" with his dog at his heels. The capitalisation could have been sarcastic, but instead comes across as fond or loving, as though recognising that his father took pride in his clothing. Causley's mother is also depicted in an idealised way with a "sprigged dress" and "straw hat" suggesting that she too has taken care for this event and is at her best. She is associated with light colours, wheat and the light of the sun, which creates an innocent impression of the scene.

The parting in Walking Away is to some extent a painful one. Day Lewis describes the child as being "wrenched" away, using the violent verb to show how the child feels the pull of others as a strong influence. The father's own influence has become weakened as he is no longer the planet that the satellite/child orbits around but has lost his child to their friends. Even when he seeks comfort, the language is surprisingly violent – "the small scorching ordeals which fire one's irresolute clay" could refer to either his child's process of growing up or his own process of letting go. The suggestion that pain is inevitable in growth could be of comfort to him, giving him a sense of meaning in this transition.

Throughout Eden Rock it seems that Causley is struggling with his own transition, perhaps coming to terms with his impending death. The metaphor of the river to cross, drawing on Greek mythology (the rivers one must cross to the world of the dead) and the Christian allusions of baptism and cleansing, implies that he is near death and contemplating heaven. His parents "beckon" to him, suggesting the comforting thought of being reunited with lost loved ones. The scene is also idyllic, with his father "leisurely" skimming stones and the idealism of the picnic and its gentle rural portrayal. Yet Causley is not entirely convinced. His final line ("I had not thought it would be like this") is separated from the others. While the previous three-line stanzas could indicate the unity of the three in the family, echoing the imagery of the "three suns", the last individual separation along with the negative introduces a note of doubt and uncertainty, perhaps inevitable at the moment of death.

Throughout Walking Away, Day Lewis is attempting to come to terms with the distance opening up between himself and his child and turns to religion to seek comfort. He writes that "God alone could perfectly show" which suggests he has to accept that there is something he cannot understand and must simply trust that everything will work as it should. The regularity of the ABABA rhyme scheme perhaps also suggests this sense of structure and planning, which Day Lewis believes underlies our lives even if we cannot see the reasoning behind it.

For both poets, the relationship between parents and children is complex. Parents both support and encourage and are inevitably separated from their children when they reach adulthood. For their part, the children are often unaware of the pain this might cause their parents, until they have been 'let go' to find their own way.

Compare how poets present ideas about love and nature in "Love's Philosophy" and "Winter Swans."

With very different approaches, both Sheers and Shelley nonetheless explore the reflection of love in the nature that surrounds them. Shelley's typically Romantic syllogism uses nature to persuade the object of his affection into a relationship, while Sheers projects his internal conflict over the state of his relationship onto the nature that surrounds him.

In Love's Philosophy, Shelley uses patterns in the natural world to persuade his love into a relationship with him. It could be seen as joyously, excessively romantic but the persuasive nature of it also has an underlying manipulative tone. He describes nature as ever-increasing, from "fountain" to "river" to "ocean", a metaphor for the potential increase in the passion in their relationship. He also portrays everything in nature as part of a couple. The "mountains kiss high heaven", waves "clasp one another", and "sunlight clasps the earth". The elements also represent this romantic partnership. Classical imagery depicts air and water as feminine, earth and fire as masculine – blending these together in his pairings suggests that the male and female belong together. Shelley's repeated use of partnerships depicts love, romance and togetherness as inevitable and, therefore, implies that any refusal of a partnership is somehow against nature.

Rather than using the external world to change his lover's internal passions, Sheers sees the couple's troubled relationship reflected in the world around him. The opening pathetic fallacy is agonisingly brutal as the waterlogged earth is "gulping for breath", fighting for survival following the storm in which the "clouds had given their all." This phrase could represent the intensity of an argument, or that the couple, too, have given everything they can and are now spent and empty. Standing at the edge of a lake, which is closed in and unmoving, they are "silent and apart", unable to communicate and resolve their differences.

Love's Philosophy presents an idealised, romanticised view of love and sex as being a transcendental experience as the elements "in one another's being mingle." This phrase, echoing the "mingling" of water at the beginning, suggests that passion creates a joining together and becoming entirely one with each other, indistinguishable. This intensity, however, could also be seen as potentially frightening, threatening to subsume one's individuality in the heated passion of a sexual relationship. Shelley's use of Romantic natural imagery takes on a greater significance given Shelley's advocacy for free love, positioning love and sex as unnaturally confined by the human religious institution of marriage. His syllogistic structure ends with the final rhetorical question "what are all these kissings worth/if thou kiss not me?" This places the responsibility for being natural or unnatural firmly on the object of his desire. If she "disdains" him like the flower, she is being decidedly unnatural.

The extended metaphor of the swans represents an effort to understand the couple's relationship, but it is a problematic comparison. They are in constant, uncertain, motion. Although they move "in unison" at times, they "halved themselves" then are "boats righting in rough weather". Like the couple, they move together and then apart, constantly tearing themselves from one another then being propelled back. The descriptions of them are equally complex. "Porcelain" is delicate and easily broken, suggesting the fragility of the couple's tentative reconciliation. "Icebergs of white feather", however, juxtaposes the softness of feathers and the hardness of ice to suggest their internal conflict. "Iceberg" could also represent the difficulties the couple have understanding one another, as they are notorious for having very little of themselves above the surface compared with their immense hidden depths. This could also signify the depth of feeling, and the difficulty they have in expressing it to one another.

The forms of both poems reflect their poets' attitudes to love. Here, too, Shelley uses ideas of a natural partnership through his combination of feminine and masculine endings balancing the first stanza much as his relationship with his intended would balance. Yet the poem becomes more masculine and insistent through the second stanza. Shelley's verb choices also become more passionate, more forceful. In the first stanza, he uses "mix" and "mingle", soft-sounding actions which are almost passive in their joining together (although this does create a sense of inevitability as no force is required – the effort would be in stopping this happening). In the second stanza there is a shift in tone and the elements "clasp" and "kiss", both more passionate and more active, suggesting the inevitable increase in the lovers' passions.

Sheer's free verse with its frequent enjambment at the start could suggest continuity, but this disintegrates once dialogue is introduced and the phrases shorten. It's significant that only the lover speaks, and the line "they mate for life" could be interpreted as hopefully optimistic, reflecting the lovers' life-time commitment. However, the provenance of this poem suggests otherwise as the collection's name, "Skirrid Hill", comes from the Welsh "Ysgariad", meaning separation or divorce. Although the poem ends with the couple holding hands the speaker merely "noticed" that they had "somehow" reached for one another and rather than feeling like a deliberate action of reconciliation this feels like consolation and grief. Rather than mating for life themselves, the swans only serve as a counterpoint to highlight the couple's failure to do the same.

For both poets, nature is crucial to a greater understanding of their relationships. Shelley uses nature consciously, even manipulatively, to persuade his lover into a passionate relationship, while Sheers sees the nature around him as a way to express his internal conflict and sadness during the ending of his marriage.

Compare how poets present romantic relationships in When We Two Parted and Love's Philosophy

Both Byron and Shelley's poems demonstrate Romantic ideals in exploring their passionate emotions. They use typically Romantic features to do so; Byron's poem borders on the gothic with its imagery of death while Shelley's focuses on nature as a way to express his feelings for his lover.

Shelley and Byron also explore relationships that were unconventional for the time in which they lived. Byron's relationship is a secret affair, as suggested in the "fame" that the lover experiences as well as the speaker's "shame". The rhyming of the two words also links the couple together. It's clear Byron cannot speak to her but must remain "in silence" rather than demonstrate his sorrow, because of the secret nature of the relationship. However, the poem's provenance suggests this might be melodramatic to the point of sarcasm. Potentially written for Lady Frances Webster, who left him to have another affair, Byron's love-life was sufficiently complex, and frequently callous, to suppose this could have been written for several lovers as a refutation of the idea that he suffered when they left. 'Mad, bad and dangerous to know', his relationship with Caroline Lamb is simply one example of the way he would enter into a passionate all-consuming relationship and then quickly move onto another, causing scandal. The rhythm of this poem could support this reading as the phrase "half-broken hearted" is suspect and by placing the rhythmic emphasis on "half", Byron undercuts the melancholy of the rest of the poem. His rhetorical question "why wert thou so dear?" seems to also imply a questioning of himself, perhaps reflecting on the passion in the relationship with a sense of confusion now that the fog of romance has lifted.

Shelley's poem can be seen as similarly unconventional in its relationship. Shelley, too, believed in free love and saw marriage as an unnatural social construct. His use of natural imagery, a typically Romantic feature, is used to create a syllogistic argument persuading his intended to be with him. The pairings in nature – "mountains kiss high Heaven", "sunlight clasps the earth" - all suggest that to be coupled is natural and, therefore, the lover is unnatural if she does not want to be partnered with someone. The balancing of masculine and feminine endings through the first stanza also hints towards this natural partnership, although as the masculine endings become more insistent in the second stanza, this perhaps implies a frustration on Shelley's part that his lover is not yet won. He, too, uses a rhetorical question to emphasise his persuasive argument. Asking her "what are all these kissings worth/if thou kiss not me?" could be read as placing blame on her for resisting and also implies that, without her, his life is not worth living.

Byron's language is at times overly formal, almost archaic. His use of "thou" and "thy" could be using the archaism to emphasise the "vows" that he and his lover have taken (although it's unclear whether it's vows to him or a husband that the lover has broken). Yet it could also be read as slightly sarcastic in its formality. He also explores the impact of time on a relationship. The sorrow continues for "long years" and he says "long, long shall I rue thee." The repetition of "long" emphasises that a relationship can have a significant lasting impact, while the word "rue" is again ambiguous - will he regret their relationship ending or it starting in the first place? He presents a sense of inevitability surrounding the relationship's failure. He writes that their break-up was "foretold" and sees, in hindsight, "the warning" that he should have heeded, looking back and seeing the signs that they would not last. The cyclical structure using the line "with silence and tears" also suggests that this ending is inevitable and should have been seen from the beginning.

Shelley uses a similar sense of inevitability in his appeal to his intended lover. The gradual increase of the elements as the "fountains", "river" and "ocean" mingle together as one suggests a force that is impossible to stop; you cannot stem the tide or stop water finding its way to the sea. He also refers to the "law divine" that pairs creatures or elements together. As Shelley was an atheist this could be knowing manipulation, alluding to a god-like divinity, or it could be the Romantic trope of elevating nature to a divine status. Either way it places pressure on the lover – a mere human after all – not to resist the divine instruction.

While both writers use dramatic and, on first reading, romantic imagery to portray their passion for their loves, both can also be read as having an unpleasant underlying tone either or mockery or manipulation. Both appear to value their own pleasures and experiences above those of their lover and use their poetry to express their superiority.

Compare how poets present changing relationships in Mother, Any Distance and Climbing My Grandfather.

In Mother, Any Distance and Climbing My Grandfather, these modern poets explore the ways that relationships change over time. In Mother, Any Distance, a new relationship is being forged as the child seeks independence by moving out but contemplates the ways that the relationship will stay the same in its love and support. In Climbing My Grandfather, Waterhouse considers the ways that understanding one another can change over time and, particularly, the way that understanding across the generations can develop.

Simon Armitage uses an extended metaphor of distance to suggest the potential gulf that can open up between parent and child when the child leaves home. He describes "acres of the walls, the prairies of the floors." These are both big open spaces which could seem intimidating, particularly the "prairies" which have connotations of adventure and discovery, of exploring a new frontier. This suggests the excitement with which a new chapter of one's life can start. However, he also uses far smaller measurements, like the "one-hundredth of an inch" that his mother measures towards the end. This in particular could suggest her desperation in trying to hold on as much and as long as she can, stretching the relationship to its breaking point.

In Climbing My Grandfather, Waterhouse also uses an extended metaphor, this time of climbing, to explore the distance between people and how the gap of understanding can be bridged. His opening line "I decide to do it free / without a net" suggests that this could be dangerous, as opening up to others often involves become vulnerable and giving up your 'safety net.' As he ascends, and becomes closer to his grandfather, he passes overhangs, "scars" and "screed". The climbing vocabulary is used to create a visual image of the grandfather, for example his "screed cheek" perhaps pockmarked, wrinkled, no longer smooth. It also works as a metaphor for the difficulties he has in developing the closeness in their relationship.

Both relationships experience moments of tension in these poems. For Armitage it is the "breaking point, where something / has to give." By separating the final clause onto its own line Armitage draws our attention to this taut moment when the relationship seems to hang in the balance, the mother and son pulling away from one another. The semantic field of space exploration also contributes as he "space walks" through the attic with his mother as the "base" to which he can always return. This demonstrates the adventure and ambition the speaker feels about moving on with their life, but it also has an undercurrent of the dangers associated with space travel. For Waterhouse, the moment of tension comes half-way when he comes across the "glassy ridge of a scar." This could be a literal scar, perhaps a memory of serious injury, or a psychological one. Either way, Waterhouse does not probe further but "gently" moves on. The wound here is already healed and to reopen it would be simply too painful – and not benefit their new relationship. This demonstrates a kind consideration, and sensitivity in Waterhouse's approach, understanding that the relationship must be on terms beneficial to both.

Both poems, too, have similarly optimistic endings. Waterhouse finds his way to the heart and mind of his grandfather, watching the "clouds" and "birds" that symbolise his thoughts and soul. There is a sense of peace, which contrasts the effort of the rest of the poem, as Waterhouse simply lies "knowing/the slow pulse of his good heart." The final line tells us that the effort has been worth it, and he feels a sense of satisfaction, even completion, in his journey to understanding. In Mother, Any Distance, the speaker has found their freedom as they "fall or fly". Although this is a conditional, ending the poem on "fly" with its open syllable is suggestive of possibility and hope rather than a plummeting fall. Perhaps the most important line of the poem might be "Anchor. Kite." This metaphor, with the imagery of flying that is echoed throughout the poem, represents the son as flying free, seeking – and finding – the adventure he seeks. "Anchor" in this context seems caring and loving. His mother is his anchor tethering him to safety – she is the safety net that he needs to enable him to take the risks he wants without fearing they will be too much for him. The caesura, rather than separating them, functions as the string between the two, an almost invisible connection that binds them together.

Waterhouse similarly uses the form and structure of his poem to represent his ideas. The free verse and long enjambed sentences reflect the way that getting to know one another and form relationships is an ongoing process, eternal as mountains seem, and that there is no one 'path' to take but everyone must find their own way up. The sentences become longer towards the end as he becomes more determined, and more able to find the closeness with his grandfather than he desires.

For both poets, the relationships with their mother/grandfather as not simple or one-sided. Rather, they are represented in a way that reflects the complexity of relationships, moving together and then apart, then back again. They explore the effort that is required to maintain close relationships, and the benefits of doing so: a warm, loving and secure mutual relationship that enables us to flourish.

Compare how poets present married relationships in 'Singh Song!' and 'The Farmer's Bride'

In Singh Song and The Farmer's Bride, the characters express passionate romantic desire for their partners, and explore the conflict that can occur between different cultures and expectations of relationships. For Singh, his bride seems perfect despite her clashing with his parents' traditional Indian behaviours, reflecting the difficult integration of many second-generation immigrants. For Mew's farmer the clash is not of culture but expectation, as his new bride behaves in ways that he finds confusing and difficult to understand.

Nagra's use of reported speech and dialect creates a verisimilitude in his poem that brings the reader into the Singhs' home. Although his customers dislike his attitude ("Hey Singh, ver yoo bin?") and call his "di worst Indian shop/on di whole Indian road" he brushes off their criticism and prefers to spend time with his wife instead. Nagra conveys a sense of mischievous pleasure in the way that Singh and his wife steal time together "ven nobody in", creating a sense that the two of them spend time together secretly, snatching moments whenever possible. Charlotte Mew also uses dialect and non-standard grammar to create a more realistic impression of her farmer; in this case the farmer is presented as honest and down-to-earth, straightforward in his language. Therefore, it highlights his confusion over his more complicated bride and the problems in their relationship. However, his description also seems to mask problems that the reader – especially a modern one – sees immediately. For example she is "all in a shiver and a scare", when she "runned away"; the alliteration and the use of shiver/scare as nouns rather than verbs calls attention to them and highlights her fear.

Nagra's male speaker appears to greatly admire his wife. He describes her as "playing wid di mouse", using the metaphor of cat-and-mouse to describe her online activities, with almost a tone of pride that she is able to outwit the men she is speaking with. That she gets "di meat" from them instead of "di cheese" also suggests that she is more intelligent than they are, able to manipulate them or persuade them into paying her more – she, therefore, seems as though she is a better businesswoman than Singh. Even the clash of cultures between his wife and parents seems to bring out Singh's admiration. When she is "effing at my mum/in all di colours of Punjabi", the range of "colours" almost suggests a tone of respect for the range of her knowledge! Interestingly, Singh uses the colloquial "effing" as a euphemism for swearing which is a decidedly English use, given that it focuses on the letter "f" which is likely not to be the swearword in Punjabi. This also demonstrates the clash of cultures, as Singh's language too has blended aspects of English with his Indian dialect. The bride, too, exhibits physical signs of the cultural clash. Her "tartan sari" is a perfect example; the Scottish tradition blended with the Indian.

In The Farmer's Bride, it is the couple who clash through their complete failure to communicate effectively. Whereas Singh sees her wife as endearing, cute and funny, the farmer is bewildered by his bride's preferences to be "out mong the sheep" and talk to the animals rather than him. Her silence is confusing for him; he expresses regret at the beginning of the poem ("too young maybe") but immediately defends himself ("there's more to do at harvest-time than bide and woo"). He describes her as a "frightened fey" which symbolises her strangeness to him, that he sees her as something other-worldly and notoriously uncontrollable. The bride is also depicted by comparison to prey animals, using the imagery of "leveret", "hare", "mouse", all wild creatures that the farmer cannot domesticate. However, unlike Singh's descriptions, which seem to be admiring, the farmer's also have connotations of recognising a disturbing vulnerability in the wife: all the images are of creatures routinely hunted by predators.

Singh expresses great physical affection for his wife, although sometimes the images might seem unusual descriptions. She has the "tummy ov a teddy;" this alliteration and the childish sound of the words almost infantilises her, suggests that her stomach is rounded and soft, but also has a tone of affection. This contrasts with her "eyes ov a gun", hard and pointed – but this also echoes the idea that she is very astute and confident, something that Singh greatly admires about her. The reference to "rowing through Putney" is a comic, open and joyful expression of sexual pleasure which is in itself quite unusual in the Anthology, where relationships tend to take a more complicated and darker turn. The ending of Singh Song! uses romanticised imagery to consolidate the impression of the couple's relationship. Sitting together alone in the store, on the "silver stool", with the peaceful quiet of the shopping centre around them, they are perfectly together. Everything about the ending is calm and romanticised; the "whispering stairs" and the "brightey moon" shining in on them, using a traditional romantic image of moonlight to picture them. Singh's final line "is priceless baby" is an indication of the depth of his romantic feeling for his bride.

For the Farmer, however, the physical attraction also takes on a disturbing tone at the end of the poem. It has become increasingly clear through his monologue that the couple has no sexual relationship and the farmer bemoans their lack of children: "What's Christmas-time without there be some other in the house than we?" Earlier, a disturbing feeling is created when the community essentially 'hunt' her down like a hare – indeed, using this simile – they "caught her, fetched her home at last/and turned the key upon her, fast", securing her inside the home. The whole society in which she lives has been a part of this, effectively telling her that she must stay with her husband in this marriage – perhaps Mew presenting the way that women in difficult and unhappy relationships become very isolated. By the end, this disturbance becomes pronounced. The emotional distance caused by the lack of understanding and communication has been compounded, and the bride "sleeps up in the attic", traditionally a servant's quarters; she has removed herself from the role of "wife" although she continues to take on the domestic chores (as we know, she has no option of leaving in her current society). At the end the farmer's physical feelings take on an obsessive quality. His exclamative "Oh! My god!" at the end is either despairing or orgasmic, fixated on "the soft young down of her" (with, again, the disturbing comparison to animals with "down"), repeating "her eyes, her hair, her hair!" passionately and desperately. At this point the reader doesn't know whether he is in the throes of misery or about to go up the stairs and physically claim his wife, but either is possible.

Although both relationships are about relative newly-weds, the Singhs are portrayed as a loving, joyous couple who take great pleasure in simply being in one another's presence. They are together navigating the world, finding their place as second-generation immigrants blending two cultures to create a new marriage. Contrastingly, Mew's farmer and bride appear utterly miserable with one another, the bride desperate to leave and the farmer desperate to stop her. Although he is unable to emotionally connect with his bride and finds her impossible to understand, he still longs for her.

Glossary – literary vocabulary

Alliteration: words close together beginning with the same letter or sound

Allusion: a reference to another story or idea e.g. the Bible

Ambiguous: open to more than one interpretation, not having one obvious meaning

Animalistic: relating to animals

Archaism: something very old or old-fashioned

Caesura: a break in the line, usually caused by punctuation

Colloquialism: everyday, slang word

Connotation: to imply a meaning or suggest something by association.

Dialect: language associated with a particular region, class or background.

Dramatic monologue: a poem spoken by a persona to an unseen listener

Echo: a repetition of sound, word, or idea.

Enjambment: when the sentence continues over the end of a line

Euphemism: a kind or pleasant way of saying something unpleasant

Extended metaphor: a metaphor that continues throughout a text.

Free verse: poetry without regular rhyme or rhythm.

Gothic: a fiction genre combining romance, horror and death

Idiom: a common phrase or saying

Imagery: visually descriptive or figurative language

Juxtaposition: two ideas placed close together to heighten the contrast

Lexis: vocabulary, the words used.

Metaphor: describing one thing as being something else

Narrative: the story of the poem

Pathetic fallacy: attributing human feelings/ responses to inanimate things, often the weather

Personification: giving inanimate objects/things human characteristics

Perspective: the viewpoint of a character

Petrarchan sonnet: a type of sonnet with a specific rhyme scheme: abbaabbacdcdcd

Phonetic: spelled how it sounds

Present participle: the -ing form of a verb, creating continuous tenses e.g. "I'm thinking"

Protagonist: the main character of a text

Provenance: place of origin

Refrain: repeated lines, often at the end of verses like a chorus

Reported speech: repeating what someone has said, rather than quoting them directly.

Rhetorical question: a question asked to create thought rather than to get a specific answer.

Rhythm: a regular repeated pattern of sound

Romantic poet: with a capital "R", relates to a period of poetry around 1800-1850, typically exploring liberty and personal feeling. Romantic poets often use the natural world to explore

Semantic field: A set of connected words.

Simile: comparing one thing to another using like or as

Sonnet: a fourteen-line poem, using iambic pentameter (ten syllables per line in an unstressed/stressed rhythm. Usually a love poem.

Stanza: a verse or set of lines

Syllable: the units into which a word is divided, e.g. "syllable" is "syll", "a", "ble."

Syllogism: a logical argument drawing a conclusion, which is sometimes invalid.

Symbol: a representation of something else.

Synaesthesia: using sense to represent one another, e.g. sounds as colours or scent as vision.

Syndetic: using conjunctions (and, because) to connect several clauses in a row

Theme: the subject or 'big idea' behind a text

Tone: the quality, emotion or mood of writing.

Transition: changing from one state or idea to another.

Triplet: three ideas, clauses, or words in a row.

Trope: a recurrent theme, often typical to a particular genre or style

Verb: a doing or action word.

Verisimilitude: the appearance of being true or real

Volta: a change of theme or idea, usually in a sonnet, at line 6 or 8.

REVISION TASK:

Identify which of the glossary words are unfamiliar

Make flashcards to learn these and practise using them in writing.

Glossary – interpretive vocabulary

Advocate: support or recommend something.

Agony: extreme mental or physical suffering.

Autobiographical: story of one's own life.

Contemporary: at the time something was written. E.g. Byron's contemporary audience is the early 1800s.

Conventional: what is generally done, believed or thought – ordinary.

Convey: to communicate, make an idea or feeling known.

Expansive: covering a wide area, extensive

Fulfilment: the sense of achieving something

Grim: very serious or gloomy

Hindsight: understanding of a situation or event only after it has happened

Idolatry: extreme admiration, love, or reverence for something or someone

Insurmountable: too great to be overcome

Longevity: long life or existence

Macabre: disturbing because concerned with or causing a fear of death

Manipulate: handle /control in a skilful manner.

Modern: Now, e.g. the modern audience response compared with the contemporary.

Morbid: an abnormal or unhealthy interest in disturbing events, particularly death.

Mournful: feeling, expressing, or inducing sadness, regret, or grief.

Nostalgia: a sentimental longing or wistful affection for a period in the past.

Nurturing: help or encourage the development of.

Ominous: giving the worrying impression that something bad is going to happen

Patriarchy: a male-dominated system of society or government

Paucity: the presence of something in only small or insufficient quantities or amounts

Plaintive: sounding sad and mournful

Prevalence: being common, frequently found

Progressive: happening or developing gradually or in stages

Prosaic: commonplace; unromantic

Refute: prove (a statement or theory) to be wrong or false

Stark: sharply, or unpleasantly, clear

Trait: a distinguishing quality or characteristic

Transformed: making a marked change in form or nature

Turbulent: characterised by conflict, disorder or confusion.

Universal: relating to or done by all people

Vicious: deliberately cruel or violent.

Virile: characterized by strength and energy

Answers:

THE POETRY EXAM

Section 1: What are the exams?

1. Lit, paper 2, section B
2. 45 minutes
3. The question, the list of poems, and one complete poem from the anthology for you to write about.
4. Between 2-3 sides.
5. 5 minutes planning, 40 minutes writing
6. Thoughtful, developed, examined.

Section 2: The mark-scheme

1. AO1 – writing style and structure; understanding the themes and ideas of the poems **(Style and ideas)**. AO2 – analysis of methods including language, structure and form. **(Analysis of methods)** AO3 – exploration of context (literary, social and historical) as well as theme. **(Context)**

2. A series of point-evidence-explanation paragraphs.
3. A structured argument or concept to prove.
4. Focusing on theme rather than technique; improved precision of interpretive language; looking at the poem as constructed; working by idea rather than chronologically.
5. A theme or idea to explore, then how the writer has approached it.
6. Look at patterns across the poem, the techniques used in different places, and impact of word choice.

Section 3: what to look for in poetry

1. Read – Find the change – Slow – Zoom – Rhyme/Rhythm – Patterns
2. Change it - Crunch it – Split it

Section 4: Analysing metaphor

Poem	Metaphor	Interpretation	Poem	Metaphor	Interpretation
WWTP:	Cold	Isolation, loneliness.	NT:	Winter	Isolation, dying like nature.
	Death	End of relationship		Sun	Corrupted symbol – cursed.
WS:	Winter	Isolation, death of relationship	S29:	Trees	Strength, permanence.
	Water	Movement, some hope.		Nature	Growth and regeneration of self
SS:	Moon	Romance	WA:	Nature	Youth / vulnerability
	Light	Intimacy, romance		Weather	Changing season = changing relationship
LP:	Nature	Inevitable growth of love	F:	Nature	Permanence; human expertise
	Water	Life-giving, feeding the relationship		Sea	Adventure, exploration
FB:	Seasons	Changing relationship in tune with nature	MAD:	Space travel	Exploration, adventure, distance.
	Animals	Bride's vulnerability		Physical distance	Emotional distance
PL:	Trees	Opening darkness, misery & violence	CMG:	Nature – climbing	Understanding grandfather
	Light (fire)	Promise of relationship but dangerous		Birds circling	Thoughts / feelings

BYWM:	Colour	Red = passion, happiness, love	ER:	Water	Death, crossing over
	Light (stars)	Glamour, romance.		Light	Nostalgia, beauty
LY:	Light	Romance, love, warmth of feeling			
	Spring	Hope for relationship			

Section 5: What is context?

1. Historical, thematic, social.
2. As a final unrelated comment in a paragraph; without linking to the text

ACADEMIC WRITING

Section 6: Improving your essay writing

1. They need separate practice, because writing practice often needs to be slower and more deliberate.
2. Literary, and interpretive

Section 7: Writing an introduction

1. It makes writing purposeful and helps paragraphs flow.
2. Naming both poems; linking by theme; focusing on writers' purpose; mentioning context; using interpretive adjectives.
3. Summarise the poem's ideas into one sentence.

Section 8: What is academic register?

1. Tone or formality of writing.
2. 3 of: using writers' surnames; using writing techniques e.g. triadic structure; using adjectives; avoiding the word quote; using interesting connectives; using synonyms for 'shows' or 'writes'; using subordinate clauses.
3. Reducing the word count but not losing the content – forcing me to write more succinctly.
4. Reduce the word count by 20%; Change your sentence starters.
5. A paragraph at a time.

Section 9: How to embed quotations

1. When the quote is fluently incorporated into a sentence and doesn't 'stick out'.
2. A word or two at a time; a short list between hyphens; at the end after a colon.

Section 10: Comma splicing

1. When two independent clauses are joined by a comma.
2. A semi-colon or full stop.

3. Replacing comma with a word or rephrasing the sentence
4. a. Sheers writes that his love is like "swans." This extended metaphor shows their love is never-ending.
Sheers' extended metaphor of the "swans" shows their love is never-ending.
Sheers writes that his love is like "swans;" through his extended metaphor he shows their love is never-ending.
b. Hardy describes standing by the "pond." It is clear that the water is stagnant like their relationship.
By describing standing by the "pond," Hardy shows that the water is stagnant like their relationship.
Hardy describes standing by the "pond", indicating that the water is stagnant like their relationship.

Section 11: Writing conclusions

1. Compare the tones of the poems; use the wording of the question
2. Introduce new ideas; analyse language; repeat yourself
3. What their common themes are; the final overall impression of the named poem linked to the question; the final overall impression of the comparison poem linked to the question.

Section 12: How to structure the perfect paragraph

1. They have an idea, a quotation, and language analysis.
2. Writer - Technique – Purpose – Explore
3. Gives you a wider range to discuss – looking at patterns is a higher-level skill – it helps you see the tone or structural change across the poem.
4. A way of making paragraphs seem like they belong together.
5. By linking the last sentence of one to the first sentence of the next through language or idea.

REVISION GUIDANCE

Section 13: How to quick-plan

1. Choose the comparison – 3-5 paragraph topics – analysis notes – introduction – conclusion.
2. Choose pairs that have something in common but differ in their presentation.
3. Either both in the same paragraph, or in smaller paragraphs that go back and forth.
4. On the exam paper – it doesn't get marked but you can use a page to plan.

Section 16: How to revise

10. Knowing the poems and knowing how to write about them.
11. 3 of: flashcards, visual/dual coding; write introductions; mind-map quotations and analysis; listen to essay plans; do a five-minute fill; annotate a blank copy of the poem.
12. Look/cover/write/check; ask someone to quiz you; who's in the bag; learn both size; the Leitner method.

One-page summaries

WHEN WE TWO PARTED – LORD BYRON

Context

Early 1800s Romantic – prizes feeling above all else
Byron notorious for affairs and scandal

RELATIONSHIP:

A lover mourns the break-up of a secret, illicit relationship (**not a death!**), dreading seeing her again and the pain it'll cause.

LANGUAGE:

Imagery of cold

"cold/Colder thy kiss"   "Sank chill on my brow"   "a shudder"

Rhetorical questions

"Why wert thou so dear?" "how should I greet thee?" → plaintive, miserable, perhaps angry with lover

Hints at an illicit affair

"I hear thy name spoken / and share in its shame"

"They knew not I knew thee / Who knew thee too well" → nobody knew about them?

Imagery of death and destruction

"half broken-hearted / to sever for years"   "I grieve"

"Pale grew thy cheek and cold"   "A knell in my ear"

The relationship has ruined them both, his life and her reputation.

The speaker seems to blame her – "thy spirit deceive"

Conspiracy of silence

Unable to speak of the relationship (fear, shame, hurt) – "in silence I grieve", "With Silence and tears", "In secret we met", "Long shall I rue thee / Too deeply to tell"

FORM AND STRUCTURE

- Cyclical structure – no hope of improvement/change
- Dramatic monologue – addressing the lover he can't see again; emphasises his misery and confusions

Great to compare:

Porphyria's Lover Relationships and death

Neutral Tones End of relationship

Farmer's Bride Relationship breakdown

"thy" – blames her for the end of the affair

"Pale grew thy cheek and cold,

Caesura/repetition → tone of disbelief, maybe anger.

Imagery of coldness and death symbolising the end of the relationship

Violent sound of "sever" – blames her, sees her as deceptive and unkind

Cyclical "silence and tears" suggests no end to the pain

In silence and tears
Half broken-hearted
To sever for years

Why only 'half' broken hearted? Is he being melodramatic? (quite a Romantic trait)

Broken / shame → illicit relationship nobody else knows. He can't confide in anyone or get comfort from anywhere.

"thy" addresses her directly (dramatic monologue) – tone of disbelief and accusation

Thy vows are all broken
…
I hear thy name spoken
And share in its shame

"Vow" – a serious promise, as good as married. Religious connotations – heightens the serious nature of the relationship

LOVE'S PHILOSOPHY – PERCY BYSSHE SHELLEY

RELATIONSHIP:

The speaker persuading the listener to become involved in a relationship. Presented as a natural outcome.

LANGUAGE

Language of nature

"fountains mingle with the river"   "mountains", "waves", "sunlight clasps the earth"   "moonlight kiss the sea"

Increasing in size

The natural elements increase – fountain, river, ocean – suggesting the inevitable growth of love

Balance of masculine and feminine

The first elements are water – associated with the feminine. Then, moves onto earth the masculine. By balancing them and putting them together, the male/female elements of the relationship are baanced, too. Likewise the sunlight.moonlight, earth/sea are all about balance and partnership – perfect harmony.

Rhetorical question to end each stanza

"What is all this sweet work worth / If thou kiss not me?" Persuasive feature; plaintive tone; ivites a response from the listener

Context

Romantic poet early 1800s. Explores sensation / emotion, often using natural imagery

FORM AND STRUCTURE

- Pastoral tradition – using nature to explore love, making romance seem natural and elevated
- Feminine / masculine rhyming – becomes more masculine towards the end, symbolising more determination to get the kiss he wants.
- Dramatic monologue - insistent

Great to compare:

Sonnet 29 – language of nature to express love

Neutral tones – contrasting nature used to express life/death

---

The elements get <u>bigger</u> through the list, suggesting the natural increase in love.

Contrast water and earth – feminine and masculine elements -suggest balance and

Argument structure – if all things in nature are together, we should be too.

The fountains mingle with the river

Language of togetherness e.g. "mingle" repeated throughout

Religious language suggests love is God's will – can't be refused

Nature is designed to be partnered – persuasive metaphor.

**Nothing in the world is single, All things by a law divine
In one another's being mingle**

Syndetic structure (use of 'and' in listing) – develops argument, and metaphorically suggests natural progression of relationship

Soft-sounding, romantic verbs e.g. "kiss", "clasp", "mix", "mingle"– gentle, loving

Links light (sun and moon) with other elements; everything in nature wants them to be

And the moonbeams kiss the sea

PORPHYRIA'S LOVER – ROBERT BROWNING

Context

Gothic influences – mix of horror and romance. 1836

RELATIONSHIP:

Porphyria and the lover have a secret relationship – she has to leave somewhere else to be with him. He longs for her visits but is jealous of her time; he strangles her to keep her with him always: the poem ends with them sitting together, her head on his shoulder.

LANGUAGE

Pathetic fallacy

"The sullen wind was soon awake/It tore the elm tops down for spite" – she "made the cheerless grate blaze up" – the misery of the lover disappears when she arrives but he knows it will be brief. "she shut the cold out, and the storm."

Objectification

"The smiling rosy little head" – once dead, Porpohyia's an "it" not a real woman.

Alliteration

"Blushed bright beneath my burning kiss": Plosive alliteration suggests passion, and violence breaking free.

Representation of women

Porphyria's gloves suggest a higher status. She "let the damp hair fall", an intimate and possibly seductive act but he strangles her with it, indicating punishment for sexual immorality. She is "too weak"

FORM AND STRUCTURE

- Dramatic monologue conveys the speaker's madness and self-justification
- Slow, deliberate pace revealing the murder
- Death revealed around half-way through
- ABABB rhyme scheme – asymmetrical, suggesting

Great to compare:

Farmer's Bride- dramatic monologue of jealousy.

Winter Swans/Neutral Tones – pathetic fallacy and doomed relationship

---

"that moment" – frozen in time by his action – justifying himself

Conflation of beauty and goodness

"Fair", "pure", "good" – all a Victorian woman should be. Porphyria isn't – having an affair – and is punished by death

Repetition of "mine" highlights his possessive nature

That moment she was mine, mine, fair. Perfectly pure and good:

Self-justification: she loves him and wants to be with him forever.

"gained" – to be together, to be in love, presented as most valuable even than life itself.

She shut the cold out and the storm, And kneeled and made the cheerless grate

Pathetic fallacy – storm's angry, vicious- like the lover. Porphyria brings joy and happiness, but briefly

"blaze" – passionate, vibrant but burns out quickly

"cheerless" – without her he's miserable

I, its love, am gained instead!

"it's" – dehumanises Porphyria, focusing on *elements* of her body rather than her person

Putting "I" first makes his desires all-important. Presumes to know her mind

SONNET 29 – I THINK OF THEE! ELIZABETH BARRETT BROWNING

Context

EBB was an invalid and wrote love letters and poems to Robert Browning (who wrote Porphyria's Lover!) When they married, her family disowned her. Themes of nature to symbolise romance

RELATIONSHIP

Parted lovers; the woman writing a response to the man's implied question "Do you think of me?"

LANGUAGE

Imagery of nature "My thoughts do twine and bud/about thee, as wild vines about a tree" "the straggling green that hides the wood" The speaker's often the climbing vine or leafy branch, with her lover being the strong tree trunk – maybe reference to her illness and feeling dependent on him for support. Suggest the wildness of her thoughts becoming passionately uncontrolled when she thinks of her lover.

Exclamative: "I think of thee" and "Who art dearer, better!" both show intensity of feeling and the desire of the speaker to let her listener know how wrong he is to be insecure.

"Burst, shattered, everywhere" – relating to the bands of greenery around the tree; throw off the difficulties of their relationship – she wants to see him in person

Religion or virility? Does the "set thy trunk all bare" with its link to the "palm tree" suggest religion – the palm tree's often used ceremonially, especially as Jesus enters Jerusalem. Or is she suggesting she wants to see his body?

FORM AND STRUCTURE

- Sonnet – traditional love poem. EBB wrote these privately to Robert Browning, not intending to publish them – so they're more intimate.
- Speeds up at "drop heavily" increasing the sense of passionate feeling, creates movement, motion and noise
- Caesura throughout → breathlessness

Great to compare:

The Farmer's Bride (passionate, romantic)

Neutral Tones - Natural imagery

Porphyria's Lover (passionate, subversive)

my thoughts do twine and bud About thee, as wild vines, about a tree.

Language of nature

The wild passion of her thoughts, the naturalness of them, the way that she feels dependent on him.

Movement – drop, burst, shatter -noise suggests strength of ...

let these bands of greenery which insphere thee / Drop heavily down, – burst, shattered, everywhere!

Triadic structure increase pace and passion

Caesura → breathlessness

Too passionately in love to think straight / being near him makes her unable to think properly. Repeated caesura.

I do not think of thee – I am too near thee.

Echoes opening; cyclical – suggesting an unrequited passion?

NEUTRAL TONES – THOMAS HARDY

RELATIONSHIP:

A speaker, remembering the end of a relationship.

LANGUAGE

Pathetic fallacy

"the sun was white, as though chidden of God" The dark grey pond is cold, dead and wintry – like the relationship.

Nature: "starving sod", leaves "fallen from an ash and were grey", - The death of nature, "Ominous bird a-wing" contrasts with the usual imagery of birds as symbolic of hope

Repetition of death "Starving sod", "the smile on your mouth was the deadest thing", - the metaphorical death of the relationship reflected in the environment around them

Colour – grey and white dominate – the colours of winter, and of blankness of feeling much as he feels now.

Context

Later Victorian. Written before he married
Themes of nature to symbolise loss
Lyric poem – expressing intense emotions

FORM AND STRUCTURE

- Cyclical structure – begins and ends at the pond with grey leaves → the inevitability and hopelessness of the relationship's end.
- Regular structure – four-line stanzas, regular rhyme scheme – to suggest the monotony of the relationship
  1. Could also suggest he's trying to control emotions
- Irregular rhythm and caesura – emotion is uncontrollable e.g. God-curst sun → difficulty

Great to compare:

Winter Swans (ending relationships)
The Farmer's bride

Colours of grey/white → death of winter

We stood by a pond that winter day, // And a pond edged with grayish leaves.

Cyclical structure → hopelessness, unending, futile

The smile on your mouth was the deadest thing / Alive enough to have strength to die;

Antithesis of death/alive – then the finality of returning to die again, symbolising the inevitable death of the relationship.

Contrasts with other poetry's more hopeful symbolism

Like an ominous bird a-wing

Imagery of bird more unusual; connotations of death and dislike

THE FARMER'S BRIDE – CHARLOTTE MEW

RELATIONSHIP

Relatively new marriage; the farmer's unrequited love for the bride is a painful experience. Although we don't hear her voice, she seems fearful of the relationship – maybe the farmer himself.

LANGUAGE

Natural imagery for the bride – presents her as tiny, vulnerable, prey creature. Wild nature compared with farmer's domesticated animals. "flying like a hare" "like a mouse" "young larch tree" "wild violets"

Colours reflect passing seasons

"oaks are brown", "blue smoke", "low grey sky", "black earth" – dark, dull colours as winter comes on – the cold loneliness of the farmer. "berries redden up to Christmas time" but It's disappointing rather than joyful

Final repeated exclamatives – symbolises his passionate desire: "her eyes, her hair, her hair!". Is he going to do anything about it?"

Irregular grammar captures the farmer's voice, creates a sense of personality: "she runned away". The farmer's perspective through verbs such as "I chose" – how much did she know the realities of marriage? Naïve bride

.

Context

Late Victorian (end 1800s)
Dramatic monologue
Themes of nature
Economics of marriage

FORM AND STRUCTURE

- Dramatic monologue – we see his perspective. She's denied a voice – her perspective is unclear.
- Passing of time/ seasons – language of years and seasons suggests this problem will continue onwards.
- Irregular stanza structure; is emotions are untamed, almost as though he's working out how he feels.

Great to compare:

Porphyria's Lover (unrequited love, possible violence at the end here)

Letters from Yorkshire – bluff, natural farmers unable to communicate with women outside their experience

---

natural imagery / anthropomorphism

"flying like a hare"
"like a mouse"
"wild violets"

Similes

usually small – hare, mouse – creatures that are preyed on.

Wild, untameable – farmer doesn't know how to approach her, unlike his farm animals.

Colour – bright contrast to the dark blues/pale greys of different seasons. Emphasises his lack of happiness.

Berries redden up to Christmas time
What's Christmas be without there be
some other in the house but we?

Christmas – irony: should be joyful, family oriented but he's lonely, and they have no children.

Rhetorical question – hopeless, despairing. Unrequited love.

She sleeps up in the attic there

Alone, poor maid.

Stanza break highlights couple's separation

"poor"- sympathetic to her. How sympathetic to him are you?

"maid" – young, implies virginal.

Attic – traditional servants' rooms; she's put herself in that position rather than wife of the house.

WALKING AWAY – C. DAY LEWIS

RELATIONSHIP

Father looking back on his relationship with son at a key moment the first time perhaps the child chooses his friends over his father without looking back.

LANGUAGE

Natural imagery of the child

"a half-fledged thing set free" – like a bird, struggling to fly the nest "Like a winged seed loosened from its parent stem". Both images suggest attempts to separate from father, but some element of chance rather than being in control

Difficulty of finding one's way in the world

"Like a satellite/Wrenched from its orbit" – simile suggests "drifting", unwillingness – "wrenched" is almost violent, the pain of separation but this is the father projecting onto the child.

Language of uncertain movement – "eddying", an uncertain gait, hesitant, loosened.

Separation of parent/child

Tone of nostalgia, perhaps regret – "Letting go" is more final; does the separation only grow with time?

The poem is "roughly/saying" – no central image as the poet struggles to find ways to capture his feelings. .

Context

Modern poet. Written for his son, remembering a key childhood moment. Language of nature paired with religion

FORM AND STRUCTURE

- Personal first person narrative – an individual relationship being presented as universal.
- Regularity of stanzas – an inevitability.
- Opening "eighteen years ago" – but NOT at birth; 18 usually "adult" age; here it must be another occasion prompting his nostalgia.
- Last line – "letting go" – nostalgia, resignation, the child growing up.

Great to compare:

Mother, any Distance (parents/children growing apart)

Follower (Parent/child relationship using natural themes/imagery)

Suggest father is the gravitational pull of early life; the "orbit" is now broken.

Like a satellite wrenched from its orbit

Violent verb – difficulty of separation. Doesn't sound voluntary – poet's view rather than child's action?

Simile shows distance, perhaps also deliberately modern image contrasting with natural imagery elsewhere

Continuing nature imagery **a half-fledged thing set free**

Half – not quite ready but on his way

Set free – finding independence.

Eddying – drifting, calm but uncertain – no path in mind.

Seed – possibility, will plant and grow, flourish

That hesitant figure, eddying away

Like a winged seed

Hesitant – unsure throughout. Or is that father's view only, reluctant to let go?

LETTERS FROM YORKSHIRE – MAURA DOOLEY

RELATIONSHIP:

A long-distance relationship, between a couple where the female speaker is working in London and the man remains in Yorkshire.

LANGUAGE

Spring imagery

"planting", "first lapwings return", "seasons / turning" → man's character is natural, down to earth – "how things are" describes his personality too, matt-of-fact. Spring symbolises new beginnings, growth.

Cold semantic field

"breaking ice on a waterbutt" - as well as the season, perhaps difficulties (long-distance) being overcome by action.

Contrast of characters

"heartful of headlines/feeding words onto a blank screen" – her job contrasts; more ephemeral. BUT language is very nurturing.

Rhetorical question – is she sad he doesn't understand her? Could relate to previous arguments.

Romanticising communication methods

"pouring air and light into an envelope", "our souls tap out messages" → almost mythical imagery suggests the heightened romance, contrasting earlier "it's not romance".

Context

Contemporary poet. Works as a journalist, has often divided time between Yorkshire and London. Journalism contrasted with nature.

FORM AND STRUCTURE

- Free verse – mode modern style reflective of everyday speech; the poet's internal, personal thoughts being expressed
- Enjambment – everyday conversational style. No hesitation: comfortable together.
- Direct address – mimics letter form

Great to compare:

The Farmer's Bride – similar masculine characters; difficulties of relationships
Winter Swans – contemporary, uses nature to explore difficult relationships

---

Alliteration – "heartful" suggests love, care, responsibility.

"words…blank screen" – communication semantic field.

Half-rhyme "word"/"world" forms a connection between speaker and lover.

heartful of headlines
feeding words onto a blank screen

"feeding…blank" – language of nurture; she grows and cares for things as much as he does – just different things.

Demonstrates trouble communicating and importance of it.

it's you
who sends me word of that other world
pouring air and light into an envelope

"pouring air and light" – romanticises their communication / relationship.

Beautiful optimistic metaphor

Direct address throughout; she's trying to explain her thoughts to him and argue that they are both doing

he saw the first lapwings return and came
indoors to write to me

Semantic field of nature associated with Yorkshire

Communication methods – writing in different ways throughout.

Lapwing symbolises spring, new beginnings

Represents his love for her; he wants to share his experience.

EDEN ROCK – CHARLES CAUSLEY

RELATIONSHIP Adult child, looking back with nostalgia at his parents, who are now dead.

LANGUAGE

Prosaic, everyday objects to symbolise characters

Parents – "ribbon in her straw hat", "HP Sauce bottle, a screw/of paper for a cork", "tin cups painted blue" → recalls not one specific occasion but lots of family days out, a sense of nostalgia through the items and therefore for the people associated.

Calm, peaceful

Contributes to the nostalgia tone – Causley looks on the relationship as still being significant. Ages "twenty-five", "twenty-three" → parents are youthful, vibrant, not aged. Father "spins…leisurely", slow verb/adverb suggesting lazy enjoyment of a beautiful day.

Possible imagery of death

"Leisurely / They beck to me from the other bank", "Crossing is not as hard as you might think". Lethe – river in Greek mythology associated with forgetting, because you cross it on the way to the world of the dead. Rivers/crossings often symbolise dying.

Context

Modern poet, often uses everyday prosaic images to convey his emotions and experiences.

Cornish – a sense of light, freshness, countryside often attributed to his location.

FORM AND STRUCTURE

- Half-rhyme throughout – sense of unreality, almost ghostlike.
- Enjambment creates an impression of continuity despite the circumstances.
- Regular stanzas but final one is divided; family now together, or unfinished sound?

Great to compare:

Before You Were Mine / Follower – Nostalgia for parental relationships.

Neutral Tones – compare ended relationships, with very different memories of the experience.

Ghosts from past comforting in moment of death?

Exclamative dialogue – reassuring from parents; here for him even now.

'See where the stream-path is!' Crossing is not as hard as you might think

Lethe – river of forgetfulness, world of dead associations.

"Eden" – connotations f paradise. "Eden Rock" is Cornish landmark, a beauty spot.

They are waiting for me somewhere beyond Eden

Narrative quality – like Before You Were Mine photograph?

The sky whitens as if lit by three suns.

Three suns – the three in the family together, symbolically reunited.

Euphemism "crossing", idea of crossing over, passing on.

Colour brightness – purity, light, bright. Heaven?

Simile suggest uncertainty – is he seeing / understanding what he thinks?

"Waiting" – peaceful, patient, calm → supportive and loving.

Comfort of seeing loved ones after death.

FOLLOWER – SEAMUS HEANEY

RELATIONSHIP:

Son looking back nostalgically at relationship with his father, considering the way their relationship has changed since he was a child.

LANGUAGE

Description of the father linked with sailing

Father is "globed like a full sail" – strong, brisk, active and forceful. "set the wing" – direct, determined. "sod rolled over without breaking" – wave metaphor suggests father in control "Mapping the furrow": he has mastery. "hob-nailed wake" – continues the wave metaphor; also the symbolism of shoes – rough, practical, enduring.

Closeness of the relationship

Emphasised through physical action; "he rode me on his back"

Verbs for walking

Changes through the poem. The boy "tripping, falling/yapping always", childish, unhelpful, very quick young gerunds. Inversion – early on it's the speaker "stumbled in his hob-nailed wake," at end father is "stumbling", signifying age / loss of decisive movement. The change in the boy following to the father as they swap places; who is the "Follower in the title?

Context

Modern poet from Northern Ireland. Rural upbringing; he often uses imagery of nature and rural farm life in his poetry.

FORM AND STRUCTURE

- ABAB rhyme scheme, with some half/close rhyme – changeable nature of the relationship; although there's an underlying stability it still changes.
- Balladesque, has four-line stanzas and regularity of rhythm: the relationship is being explored, but changing
- Iambic tetrameter mimics walking pace, like the storyline of the poem

Great to compare:

Before you were mine / Mother, Any Distance, Walking Away – child/parent relationships changing, looking back trying to understand the differences.

But today
It is my father who keeps stumbling
Behind me, and will not go away.

"But" indicates shift of tone/idea

"go away" Real or a memory?

Change of "stumbling", child to parent, shows age and role reversal

symbolises the father-practical, no-nonsense

Hard working, hard wearing.

Stumbled in his hob-nailed wake
First use of "stumbled".
"wake" is further sea imagery

Technical semantic field – in his element, understands everything even what confuses the child

Extended metaphors of sea – controlling nature elemental, primal.

His shoulders globed like a full sail strung

between the shafts and the furrow.

"globed" – bent over, hunched – physical impression, worn with work but incredibly strong

MOTHER, ANY DISTANCE – SIMON ARMITAGE

Context

Modern poet (1993)

RELATIONSHIP:

Son, moving into his first house leaving family home. Mother loving (looks after him). Speaker sees her importance, but excited about freedom.

LANGUAGE

Semantic field of distance

"Single span" "measure"   "acres" "prairies" "metres, centimetres" "one-hundredth of an inch"

Imagery of exploration

"zero-end" and "back to base" imply space travel – the speaker's "space-walk through the empty bedroom". "an endless sky / to fall or fly." Child's astronaut ambitions suggest optimism, hope, possibility

Symbolises relationship's strength

"Anchor. Kite" – the <u>caesura</u> creates a separation; "Anchor" is a point of safety but also holding back. "line still feeding out"

"breaking point" "something has to give" → the changing relationship

Movement upwards

"leaving up the stairs" "climb"   "floors" to "loft"
Implying the changing relationship as the speaker moves onto his new life and new home, the mother not quite letting go.

FORM AND STRUCTURE

- Free verse – seeking freedom
- 2 four line stanzas then a long third stanza (letting go, falling or flying)
- End: "to fall or <u>**fly**</u>" → doubt, hope, optimism. Separated on its own for finality.
- 1st & 2nd stanzas balanced between speaker and mother; 3rd stanza focuses on the "I" alone.

Great to compare:

Walking Away (parental distance)
Follower / Before You Were Mine (parent/child)

Farmer's Bride (relationship breakdown)

Semantic field of distance

"acres", "prairies", "metres", "one-hundredth of an inch"

Symbolises changing relationship – links to exploration, closeness and mother holding on

Final line separated
Metaphor for success or failure

an endless sky / to fall or fly.

Possibility and hope "endless"
Last word –"Fly" - optimism

Anchor. Kite

Kite – wants to "fly", escape and achieve

Caesura – separation yet always connected

Anchor – ambiguous. Keeping safely on the ground of holding back?

BEFORE YOU WERE MINE – CAROL ANN DUFFY

RELATIONSHIP:

Looking at a photograph, a daughter wonders what her mum's life was like before she was born, with a feeling of curiosity, maybe even jealousy.

LANGUAGE

Glamourous imagery: "dress blows round your legs. Marilyn.", "fizzy, movie tomorrows", *"Cha cha cha!"* "bold girl winking" – mother is idolised as glamourous, exciting and fun-loving. Slight hint of resentment she's not like that anymore.

Rhetorical questions: "The decade ahead of my loud, possessive yell was the best one, eh?" – adjective "possessive" shows resentment; the daughter 'owning' the mother but whose perception is this? The questions imply disappointment the mother's old self has vanished.

Triadic structures: "where you sparkle and waltz and laugh" – light joyful verbs emphasise mother's carefree attitude.

Repetition: "before you were mine." – Ending with the title; possessive pronoun "mine" might show jealousy over her mother's previous life. Trying to understand the difference.

Context

Scottish poet; reference to George Square grounds the poem, and is important in visualising the mother.

FORM AND STRUCTURE

- Direct address – prompted by photograph. Exploring the relationship
- Regular stanzas – time passes through each one; relationship moves on.
- Caesura to emphasise key words e.g. Marilyn
- Enjambment, and rhetorical questions – sounds like conversation directed at

Great to compare:

Mother, Any Distance; Follower – changing relationship with parents.

Walking Away – looking for the moment of separation in a familial relationship

---

in the ballroom with the thousand eyes, the fizzy, movie tomorrows

Thousand eyes – being watched, the centre of attention. Vaguely mythical, linking to icons throughout the poem.

Movie tomorrows – metaphor; happy ever after, but elusive and unreal.

Fizzy – exciting, unknown, the quiver in your stomach

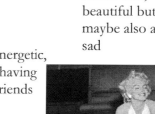

Marilyn-iconic, movie-star, beautiful but maybe also a bit sad

Red heels- passionate, sexual, youthful and vibrant.

Clatters – can't quite walk; younger trying to be grown up

Relics – reminders of something long gone

Shriek – energetic, feminine, having fun with friends

those high-heeled red shoes, relics,

and now your ghost clatters toward me over George Square

Ghost – the imagination of her young

George Square- in Edinburgh; poet's home town

shriek at the pavement.
Your polka-dot dress blows round your legs. Marilyn.

Caesura draws attention to name to emphasize glamour and unreality.

WINTER SWANS – OWEN SHEERS

RELATIONSHIP:

A couple walking; the speaker explores through metaphor their troubled relationship and wonders if it can be saved.

LANGUAGE

Pathetic fallacy

"The clouds had given their all" "the waterlogged earth / gulping for breath at our feet" – break in the storm of their relationship; temporary? Personification – gasping, drowning. Effort but is it futile?

Swan extended metaphor

"They mate for life" – like the couple? "they halved themselves in the dark water...before returning again" at the end hands have "folded, one over the other, / like a pair of wings settling after flight" – changing motion of the couple themselves; breaking up is a process not immediate. "icebergs of white feather" – juxtaposition of hard/ soft, intense cold/ feather warmth – change in couple's togetherness.

Imagery of fragility

"Porcelain" – fragile china, might break apart if too rough.

Boat / lake imagery "like boats righting in rough weather" – storm imagery; couple recovering? Lake - Movement and current unlike Neutral Tones

Context

A modern Welsh poet, still writing. Winters Swans comes from a collection exploring the

FORM AND STRUCTURE

- Free verse – more like natural speech; elements of monologue. Some halting sounds – uncertainty.
- Three line stanzas but the last has two lines – symbolises a coming together, or an unfinished question?
- Irregular fractured rhythm – shows conflict in the relationship

Great to compare:

Neutral Tones / When We Two Parted – cold wintry, end of relationship

---

they halved themselves in the dark water, icebergs of white feather

Halved – separated like the couple but come

Dark water – unknowable, potentially dangerous

Extended metaphor of swans.

Juxtaposition iceberg / feather – cold/hard, soft/warm → the constant difficult of relationship. Two opposites attracting?

the waterlogged earth gulping for breath at our feet

Pathetic fallacy of storm reflects the arguments in relationship

Personification "gulping" suggests drowning, struggling like relationship

Waterlogged – in difficulty, can't take any more.

Holding hands – subconscious reaching together; natural movement

like a pair of wings settling after flight.

Settling after a rough time

Extended swan metaphor

SINGH SONG! – DALJIT NAGRA

RELATIONSHIP:

A romantic poem about a new-ish marriage between an Indian-English couple

LANGUAGE:

Phonetic spelling / non-standard grammar

Designed to create the impression and sound of Punjabi-influenced English. "Dis dirty floor need a little bit of mop"

Contrasting imagery of British / Indian heritage

His bride wears "Tartan sari" → the combination of cultures, often second-generation

Conflict of generations

"she effing at my mum...making fun of my daddy" - contrary to stereotypes of respectful behaviour; the bride mocks his parents; drinking and swearing makes us think less of her in this situation.

Description of the bride "tiny eyes ov a gun/and di tummy ov a teddy" – sweet childish affectionate description represents his love for her.

Context

Modern poet (2007)
Published in a collection exploring Indian-English heritage – use of dialect, and modern imagery /setting

FORM AND STRUCTURE

- Free verse – less structured, more like thought or conversation.
- Uses italics to suggest speech – sometimes a customer, sometimes the speaker or his wife.
- Irregular stanza/line length – represents a more modern conversational style.
- Stanza breaks often move place e.g. upstairs, back to the shop.

Great to compare:

Walking Away (parental distance)
Follower / Before You Were Mine (parent/child)

Farmer's Bride (relationship breakdown)

Romanticised imagery – "silver" evokes starlight

"whispering" personifies; the shop wills them together

Anywhere they are is romantic, even the corner shop.

vee cum down whispering stairs and sit on my silver stool, from behind di chocolate bars

Contrasts expectation of "proper" Indian behaviour

"tartan sari"

Juxtaposed with the prosaic chocolate bars (though chocolate *also* a symbol of modern romance)

"she effing at my mum in all di colours of Punjabi"

Juxtaposition of Indian/English

Conflict of wife / parents in the relationship with the speaker

Phonetic spelling to represent accent

tiny eyes ov a gun and di tummy ov a teddy

Childish, affectionate description

Sweet, romantic – shows genuine feeling.

CLIMBING MY GRANDFATHER – ANDREW WATERHOUSE

Context

Modern poet; concerned with nature and the environment; a keen mountaineer.

RELATIONSHIP

Speaker 'climbing' grandfather, getting to know him.

LANGUAGE:

Extended metaphor of climbing

Climbing as metaphor for getting to know someone; reminiscent of childish behaviour climbing a sleeping grandad in a chair. "without a rope or net". Getting to know someone is sometimes more difficult than other times.

Physical metaphors

"skin of his finger is smooth and thick/like warm ice." "To drink among teeth" - the physical mountain functions as extended metaphor for the body and mind of the grandfather

Dangers of getting to know someone

Doesn't pry, knows what to leave: "I discover / the glassy ridge of a scar, place my feet / gently in the old stitches and move on."

Increase in pace towards end Short clauses, increasing pace from "Refreshed" onwards; the upwards climb gathers pace as he gets deeper into understanding his mind. "Watching clouds and birds circle.

FORM AND STRUCTURE

- Starts present tense "I decide" – immediacy, in the moment.
- Single stanza mimicking the movement of climbing; one action, smooth and quick.
- Irregular lines / rhythm -sometimes climbing more difficult, like getting to know someone.
- "good heart" final words; the most important knowledge.

Great to compare:

Follower / Before You Were Mine – getting to know a parental/adult figure.

I discover / the glassy ridge of a scar, place my feet / gently in the old stitches and move on

Scar – physical and emotional; risks reopening old wounds by getting to know him.

Adverb gently implies caution; won't look too hard in some places.

Extended metaphor – scar is a section of a mountain

can only lie watching clouds and birds circle, feeling his heat, knowing the slow pulse of his good heart.

Clouds/ birds – softer symbolism at the top. Hair image? Calm, peaceful.

Has been tiring but worth it

"Good heart" – rhythm at end slows. Final words emphasise the grandfather's personality; the value of the climb.

Juxtaposition "warm ice" – contradictions of grandfather but also suggests a comfort; this isn't interrogation -he is willing to be discovered.

skin of his finger is smooth and thick/like warm ice

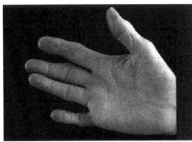

Masculinity of physical description, also shows age and hard work has worn his hands.

Printed in Great Britain
by Amazon